Bed and Breakfast Quilts

With Rise and Shine Recipes

Mimi Dietrich

Thanksgiving 2004
Trip to Wisconsin
Teresa Jamie-Cameron
& Mackenzie
Special trip over to Beaver Dam
-Nancy's Notions - Great Fun
Yoli

Martingale™
& COMPANY

Bed and Breakfast Quilts:
With Rise and Shine Recipes
© 2003 by Mimi Dietrich

Martingale & Company
20205 144th Avenue NE
Woodinville, WA 98072-8478
www.martingale-pub.com

Credits

President: Nancy J. Martin
CEO: Daniel J. Martin
Publisher: Jane Hamada
Editorial Director: Mary V. Green
Managing Editor: Tina Cook
Technical Editor: Karen Costello Soltys
Copy Editor: Karen Koll
Design Director: Stan Green
Illustrator: Laurel Strand
Photographer: Brent Kane
Cover and Text Designer: Stan Green
Recipe Development: Spectrum Communication
                              Services, Inc.
Food Photographer: Dean Tanner, Primary Image

Printed in China
08 07 06 05 04 03   8 7 6 5 4 3 2

Library of Congress Cataloging-in-Publication Data

Dietrich, Mimi.
     Bed and breakfast quilts with rise and shine recipes /
Mimi Dietrich.
          p. cm.
     ISBN 1-56477-439-2
     1. Quilting—Patterns. 2. Patchwork—Patterns.
3. Appliqué—Patterns. 4. Breakfasts. I. Title: Bed and
breakfast quilts with rise and shine recipes. II. Title.

     TT835 .D528 2003
     746.46'041—dc21

                                        2002151321

Mission Statement

We are dedicated to providing quality products
and service by working together to inspire
creativity and to enrich the lives we touch.

Dedication

To all the quilters who helped make the quilts, especially Emily Pelton Watson, my quilter's apprentice.

Acknowledgments

A year ago, this book was just a dream. With the help of wonderful friends, family, and colleagues, it is now a reality! Many thanks to:

Nancy J. Martin, who loved my idea and said the right words to encourage me to do this project.

Emily Pelton Watson, who became my quilter's apprentice in the summer of 2002 and helped piece many of the quilt tops.

Linda Newson, professional machine quilter, who added creative stitches to bring many of the quilts to life.

Monday Night Madness in Baltimore, Maryland: Joan Costello, Phyllis Hess, Barbara McMahon, Vivian Schafer, and Laurie Gregg, machine quilter.

The Vintage Quilters in Cedar Falls and Waterloo, Iowa: Shelly Cornwell, Karan Flanscha, Nancy Hayes, Barbara Jacobson, Sharri Nottger, Robin Venter, and Joyce Kuehl, machine quilter.

The Helping Hands Quilt Guild in Dover, Delaware: Kay Butler, Louise Brown, Sue Ellen Dennis, Anne Edwards, Flo Gomory, Debbie Hibbert, Janet Johnson, Cindy Mayan, Jennie Palmer, Pam Sullivan, Barb Shutz, Lauren Taylor, Joyce Wade, Rachel Hershberger, and Sarah Hershberger, hand quilters.

Jean Fries and her Amish friends, hand quilters.

Members of the Village Quilters in Catonsville, Maryland, and the Friendship Quilters in Glen Burnie, Maryland, who made yo-yos for the pillows.

Members of my Graduate Class who appliquéd basket handles: Asako Reth, Eleanor Eckman, Dori Mayer, Peggy Bonner, Kay Smith, Barbara Ditto, Mary Stewart, Jody Schatz, Pamela Budesheim, Jean Harmon, Barbara Kopf, Betty Morton, Joan Schachnuk, Barbara Bennett, Sherri Eisenstein, Polly Mello, Marylou McDonald, Anita Askins, Pat Glynn, Helen Watkins, Jan Carlson, and Kathy Suita.

Members of my Baltimore Appliqué class who appliquéd wreaths: Cheryl Sleboda, Angela Dukehart, Ann Corbett, Martha Willing, Robin Stinchcomb, Donna Norris, Jean Ann Hudson, Penny Seymore, Sue Campise, Michele McComas, Angel Burba, Valerie Simonds, Carrie Manion, Gayle Walters, and Sue Cochrane.

Norma Campbell, who designed the Spool block.

Kathy Cook, who inspired me to embroider the pillowcases.

Karen Baker, who inspired one of the quilts.

Barbara Burnham, who graciously allowed her "Welcome Home" quilt to be used in the book.

Sue Campise and Ginny Stone, who helped me find enough fabric for one of the projects.

Ursula Pelton, who helped sew accessories for the quilts.

The staff at Seminole Sampler Quilt Shop in Catonsville, Maryland, especially Robbyn Robinson, for their patience when I chose fabrics for the projects.

Arlene Chase, Pat Hersl, Helen Quane, Beth Rice, and Kay Worley, who sewed binding on the quilts.

Sue Brunt and Phyllis Hess for recipe ideas.

Maywood Fabrics for the fabrics used in "Friendship Baskets" and "Garden Comfort."

Timeless Treasures for the fabrics used in "Spring Daydreams."

Quilter's Dream Cotton for providing their "Select" cotton batting.

Mary Green, Karen Soltys, Terry Martin, and the staff at Martingale & Company.

And the best quilter's husband, Bob Dietrich.

Contents

Introduction

Have you ever spent the night at a bed and breakfast inn? It's a charming experience and entirely different from staying at a hotel. If you are looking for a relaxing getaway, a cozy vacation, or a romantic respite, a B&B is the perfect place. It might look like a wayside inn, a country cottage, or an antique mansion, but it will have all the comforts of home—and more.

Each B&B reflects the personality of the owners who live there. They greet you when you arrive, show you around, make you feel welcome, and prepare breakfast for you. They graciously offer information about places of interest and give you directions. You are truly a guest in their home. Travelers often return to B&Bs to renew friendships and acquaintances with the proprietors.

B&Bs are unique to the areas in which they're located. I have stayed in an Amish farmhouse in Lancaster County, Pennsylvania; a Victorian mansion in Cape May, New Jersey; a 1700 colonial home on the Eastern shore of Maryland; an adobe in New Mexico; and a beach house on Puget Sound near Seattle. Each place I visited, I imagined quilts to make for the beds. These experiences inspired me to write this book.

An abundance of special details such as flowers, romantic china, and vintage stitchery all serve to welcome guests.

The decorations in a B&B are unusual and interesting. Unlike in a hotel, each room is different. Many owners use antiques or furniture from the family collection to create a comfortable feeling. A quilt is usually the focal point in the bedroom, setting a comfortable tone with colors and textures. There's often a gathering room or parlor where you can read, listen to music, or watch television with

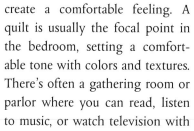

other guests. If it feels like home to you, it just might be because it is the owner's home!

Breakfast in a B&B is a social occasion. Before you arise, the owners are up early fixing breakfast. Delicious aromas wake you. Travelers gather for coffee and conversation and then start the day with a morning feast at a large table. You visit with the owners and other guests as you eat. The owners serve specialty recipes and will frequently share them with you. Often they have compiled a cookbook, knowing that visitors will ask for recipes. Although by definition most B&Bs serve only breakfast, sometimes they offer tea in the afternoon when travelers arrive.

The recipes in this book will quickly become the specialties of your house when you serve them to your guests. Try Oven-Baked French Toast for a casual breakfast or Oatmeal Crème Brûlée to serve a group of friends. Sip my Favorite Hot Chocolate to guarantee a good night's sleep and pleasant dreams.

The quilts in the book were photographed on location at a variety of B&Bs. Wouldn't it be fun to incorporate some of the special touches experienced at these inns right in your own home? If you have a guest room, or if your children have moved out, decorate your room using your favorite B&B ideas. Paint the walls a fresh new color! Rearrange your furniture in a new way. Put a new quilt on your son or daughter's old bed! Arrange a bouquet of fresh flowers on a fancy doily or a small quilt. Get a new frame for a favorite print. Dress up and display your favorite doll. Fold your grandmother's quilt on the bottom of the bed—or make a new one just for you! Your guests will be impressed with your creativity and classic sense of style.

Quilters usually have wonderful collections of sewing items and find it easy to decorate a "quilter's retreat." Wouldn't it be fun to use an antique sewing-machine table as a night stand? Stitch a small quilt or frame a favorite quilt block to hang on the wall. Use antique bobbins as candle holders, and display thimble collections on small shelves. Place a pair of fancy scissors on a doily with colorful spools of thread. For a surprising touch of color, sprinkle buttons in a small basket filled with potpourri. Use a basket to store your favorite quilting magazines. And of course, make a pieced spool quilt, "Quilter's Sweet Dreams," to put on the bed.

Mouthwatering breakfast treats are one sure way to get visitors out of a comfy, quilt-topped bed!

A travel theme is perfect for a guest room. Frame prints or postcards or photos collected in your travels. Display a collection of souvenir spoons from a variety of places—even if one of those places is your favorite antique shop! Make a quilt from fabric collected on vacation. Use a suitcase as a small table, or fill a small tote bag with books, magazines, or travel brochures.

Create a bed and breakfast room using a theme with a regional flair. A seaside room can include lighthouses, fish, a basket of seashells, and cool underwater colors. A mountain resort room might include a woodsy decor. The quilt "Starry Night" brings the night sky indoors. You can always make your guests feel comfortable with the quilt "Welcome Home."

A garden theme is always a delightful setting. Botanical prints bring a touch of the outdoors to the walls. Fresh flowers in a special vase add fragrance as well as beauty to a room. A quilt appliquéd with flowers makes it feel like summer in any season. Delight your guests with the blossoms on "Spring Daydreams" or the whimsical yo-yo flowers on "Garden Comfort."

A memorabilia room is fun to design. Cluster old photographs on an antique dresser. Hang a baby dress on a small decorative hanger. Display a scrapbook or old yearbook on a hope chest. Add new life to objects around your house by making them part of your special guest room.

Use reproduction fabrics to make "Vintage Memories" in soft antique shades.

Create a family guest room to teach your grandchildren their heritage. Frame old family photos, or put them in a special album. Group baby pictures of grownups together with photos of their children. Photos of grandparents and parents as children are certain to spark family conversations. Antique toys and rocking horses add a personal touch to the room. Include a family quilt if you are lucky enough to own one. Stitch "Count Your Blessings" for all of your family memories.

Quilts are the focal point in most guest rooms. The feeling of warmth and welcome is reflected in the colors, textures, and handmade stitches in the quilts. To help you get started in decorating a special room, this book includes a variety of ideas using patchwork designs, appliqué accents, and a combination of techniques. There are also plenty of ideas for pillows, pillowcases, shams, and other accessories to accent your style.

When you choose colors for your quilts, it's important to use relaxing, comfortable colors. Blues and greens are cool and soothing. Reds and yellows are warm. The theme of some quilts suggests appropriate colors, like yellow for "Rise and Shine" or green for "Spring Daydreams." Brown is a necessity for "Chocolates on My Pillow," but a touch of hot pink brightens the design.

Calm and soothing or purely Victorian are just two ways you could turn an ordinary spare room into a restful guest retreat.

The scale of the fabric prints should match the size of the quilt designs. Use large-scale prints and florals for quilts such as "Wish upon a Star" or "And to All a Good Night." Small prints are more appropriate for quilts with smaller pieces such as "Quilter's Sweet Dreams" or "Twilight in the Garden." Some quilt designs suggest special prints, like sewing prints in "Quilter's Sweet Dreams" or small accent prints in the appliquéd circles in "Garden Comfort."

The quilts in this book were made with standard quilter's cotton fabric that is about 42" wide. Flannels are warm and cozy and would be beautiful to sew in quilts with larger pieces such as "Wish upon a Star" or "And To All a Good Night." Lightweight, 54"-wide decorator prints would also be appropriate for these quilts.

As you design your own guest room, make sure you have a guest book. Encourage visitors to sign their names and record the dates they stay with you. It's a great way to keep a journal of the journeys! After my son Ryan moved out, he returned to spend the night in his redecorated room. The comment he wrote in the guest book the next day was priceless: "It feels like home."

Enjoy the ideas in this book, make yourself a cup of hot chocolate, light a candle, curl up under a quilt, and dream, or for special inspiration, treat yourself to a night at a bed and breakfast!

CREATE A COMFORTABLE GUEST ROOM

When it comes to helping guests feel welcome, consider including the following things in your guest room for a visit they won't forget.

- Coordinated bed quilts and pillows
- Soothing colors
- Night table next to bed
- Fresh flowers in a pretty vase
- Small quilts used as doilies
- Night-light
- Reading light
- Magazines or books
- Alarm clock—but not one that ticks
- Chocolates on the pillow
- Empty hangers in the closet or hook over the door
- Towels tied with a satin ribbon
- Specialty soaps and shampoos in a basket
- Candle with a soothing fragrance

Fresh flowers and spare quilts nearby make any room feel cozy.

A wall quilt is a perfect backdrop for a relaxing afternoon break.

Quilter's Sweet Dreams

Patchwork spools stitched in pastel colors—perfect for a quilter's guest room! When the kids move out, many quilters redecorate their rooms in "quilter chic" using thimbles, scissors, bobbins, and other sewing collectibles as accent pieces. Frame quilt blocks or stitchery for the walls, and add a basket of favorite magazines and quilt books. Use your favorite collection of fabrics to make a coordinating spool quilt! Use pink fabric for a feminine touch on the border.

Invite your quilter friends over for a pajama party and a night of sewing, laughing, and sharing great ideas. Serve Thimble Cookies with coffee in the morning to start a new day of stitching. Your guests will think of you as the perfect hostess after creating fond memories and enjoying sweet dreams in your quilter's retreat.

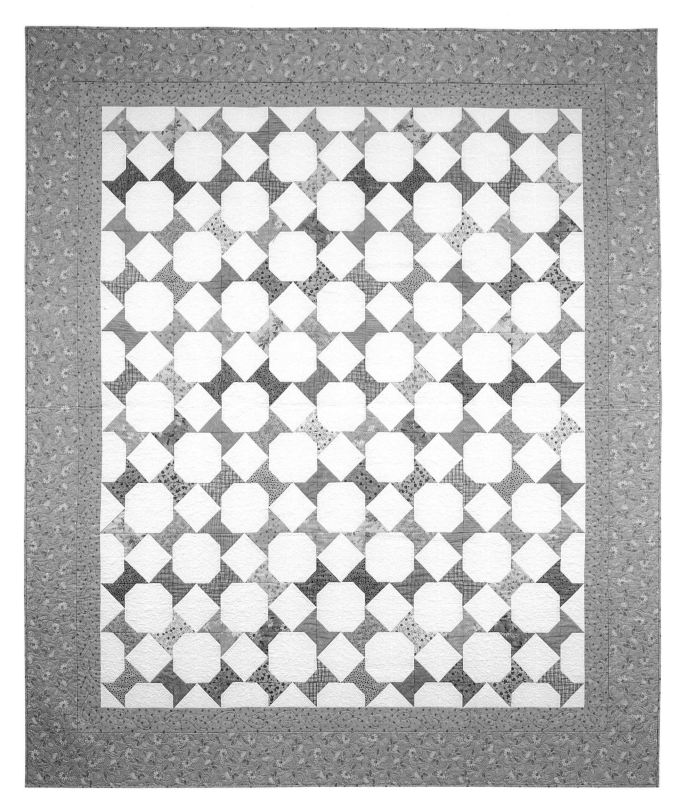

Quilter's Sweet Dreams

Block designed by Norma Campbell. Pieced by Mimi Dietrich and Emily Watson, Baltimore, Maryland, 2002.
Machine quilted by Linda Newsom, Crofton, Maryland.

Finished Quilt Size: 78½" x 90½"
Finished Block Size: 6" x 6"

Materials

Yardage is based on 42"-wide fabric unless otherwise stated.

20 fat quarters (18" x 20") of assorted pastel prints for blocks
3¾ yds. white-on-white print for blocks*
2¾ yds. green print for inner border and binding
2½ yds. pink floral for outer border
7 yds. for backing
83" x 95" piece of batting
Add 2½ yds. to make pillowcases.

Cutting

All measurements include ¼"-wide seam allowances.

From *each* of the 20 pastel print fat quarters, cut:
- 6 squares, 3⅞" x 3⅞"; cut each square once diagonally to make 12 triangles (240 total)
- 12 squares, 2" x 2" (240 total)

From the white-on-white print, cut:
- 12 strips, 3⅞" x 42"; crosscut into 120 squares, 3⅞" x 3⅞"; cut each square once diagonally to make 240 triangles
- 22 strips, 3½" x 42"; crosscut into 240 squares, 3½" x 3½"

From the green print, cut on the lengthwise grain:
- 2 strips, 3½" x 72½"
- 2 strips, 3½" x 66½"
- 9 binding strips, 2" x 42", cut on the crosswise grain

From the pink floral, cut on the lengthwise grain:
- 4 border strips, 6½" x 78½"

Making the Spool Blocks

You need 120 Spool blocks for this quilt.

1. Sew a pastel triangle to a white triangle. Press the seams toward the pastel triangle. Make 2 for each Spool block.

2. Using a pencil, draw a diagonal line on the reverse side of each 2" pastel square.

3. With right sides together, place a pastel square in the corner of a 3½" white square, aligning the raw edges as shown.

4. Sew on the marked line. Press the pastel square toward the corner to create a triangle; then trim away the bottom 2 layers, leaving a ¼" seam allowance.

Sew.   Press.

5. Arrange 4 pieced squares as shown. Sew them together to make a Spool block.

  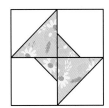

6. Repeat steps 1–5 to make 6 blocks from each pastel fat quarter, for a total of 120 blocks.

Assembling the Quilt

1. Arrange the patchwork blocks as shown. Sew the spools together in rows; and then sew the rows together.

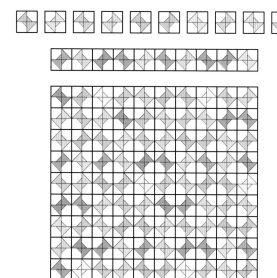

2. Sew the 3½" x 72½" green strips to opposite sides of the quilt. Sew the 3½" x 66½" green strips to the top and bottom of the quilt to complete the inner border.
3. Sew 2 of the 6½" x 78½" pink strips to opposite sides of the quilt. Sew the remaining 2 pink strips to the top and bottom of the quilt to complete the outer border.

Finishing

1. Mark the quilt top with a design of your choice.
2. Piece the backing horizontally to fit the quilt top.
3. Layer the quilt top with batting and backing; baste the layers together.
4. Hand or machine quilt as desired.
5. Trim the batting and backing even with the edges of the quilt top. Sew the green print binding to the quilt.
6. Make a label and attach it to your quilt.

PILLOW TALK

To coordinate with your "Quilter's Sweet Dreams" guest-room quilt, make spool pillowcases using the directions on page 115. Sew extra Spool blocks to the edges of the pillowcases.

Make a throw pillow using the directions on pages 115–16. Use one Spool block framed with 2½" borders as the center of the pillow. Add 3½" borders and large button embellishments to finish the pillow.

Thimble Cookies

INGREDIENTS

- 2 eggs
- ⅔ cup unsalted butter, at room temperature
- ½ cup firmly packed brown sugar
- 1 teaspoon freshly grated orange peel
- ¼ teaspoon salt
- ¼ teaspoon ground nutmeg or cinnamon
- 1 teaspoon vanilla
- 1½ cups all-purpose flour
- 1 cup finely chopped pecans or walnuts
- ⅓ to ½ cup jam or preserves (strawberry, cherry, peach, raspberry, mint, or apricot)
- Thimble (optional)

DIRECTIONS

1. Lightly grease a cookie sheet; set aside. Separate egg yolks from whites; set whites aside for coating cookie dough balls.
2. In a large bowl, beat butter with an electric mixer at medium speed for 30 seconds. Add brown sugar, orange peel, salt, and nutmeg. Beat until combined, scraping sides of bowl occasionally. Beat in the 2 egg yolks and vanilla. Using a wooden spoon, stir in flour. Cover and refrigerate 1 hour or until dough is easy to handle.
3. Preheat the oven to 375°F (190°C). Place pecans and the 2 egg whites in 2 separate small, shallow bowls. Slightly beat egg whites with a fork. Shape chilled dough into 1¼" balls. Dip each ball into egg whites, and then roll in chopped nuts to coat. Place balls about 2" apart on prepared cookie sheet. Press a thimble or your thumb into the center of each ball to make an indentation.
4. Bake 10 to 12 minutes or until the edges of the cookies are firm and lightly browned. Quickly remove from baking sheet. Cool on a wire rack. When cookies are cool or just before serving, pipe or spoon a small amount of jam or preserves (about ¾ teaspoon) into the center of each cookie. Makes about 2 dozen cookies.

Chocolates on My Pillow

When you are away from home, it's a treat to find a chocolate on a turned-down bed in your room at night. Wonderful, rich, warm, brown fabrics in the local quilt shop inspired this quilt. They all made me think of chocolates!

This little chocolate-square design is fun and easy to sew. The Nine Patch blocks are set into an arrangement reminiscent of antique woven coverlets. As you sew, try not to count the squares you are making. Instead, imagine each piece of brown fabric as a chocolate, and this quilt will be a special delight!

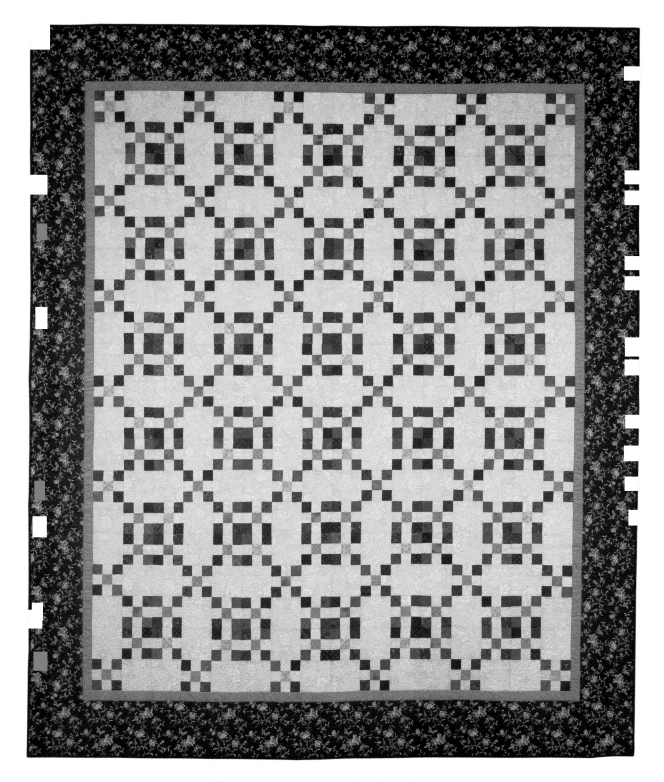

Chocolates on My Pillow

Designed by Mimi Dietrich. Pieced by Mimi Dietrich and Emily Watson, Baltimore, Maryland, 2002.
Machine quilted by Linda Newsom, Crofton, Maryland.

Finished Quilt Size: 91½" x 105"
Finished Block Size: 4½" x 4½"

Materials

Yardage is based on 42"-wide fabric unless otherwise stated.

5 yds. tan print for blocks

2¾ yds. brown-and-pink floral print for outer border★

12 fat quarters (18" x 20") of assorted brown prints for blocks

4 fat quarters (18" x 20") of assorted bright pink prints for blocks

⅝ yd. pink print for inner border

¾ yd. dark brown print for binding

8½ yds. fabric for backing

96" x 109" piece of batting

★Add 1 yard for pillow shams.

Cutting

All measurements include ¼"-wide seam allowances.

From each of the 12 brown print fat quarters, cut:
• 6 strips, 2" x 20" (72 strips total)

From each of the 4 bright pink print fat quarters, cut:
• 5 strips, 2" x 20" (20 strips total; 2 are extra)

From the tan print, cut:
• 36 strips, 2" x 42"; cut each strip in half crosswise for a total of 72 strips
• 18 strips, 5" x 42"; crosscut into 142 squares, 5" x 5"

From the pink print, cut:
• 9 strips, 2" x 42"

From the brown-and-pink floral print, cut on the lengthwise grain:
• 2 border strips, 8½" x 89"
• 2 border strips, 8½" x 91½"

From the dark brown print, cut:
• 10 binding strips, 2" x 42"

Making the Nine Patch Blocks

You need 162 Nine Patch blocks for this quilt.

1. Sew a brown strip to each long edge of a 2"-wide tan strip. Press the seams toward the brown strips. Make 36 strip sets using 72 brown strips and 36 tan strips.

   Use a ruler and rotary cutter to clean-cut the edges of the strip set. Crosscut the strips every 2" to make 324 segments.

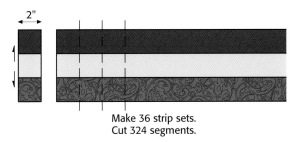

Make 36 strip sets.
Cut 324 segments.

2. Sew a 2"-wide tan strip to each long edge of a bright pink strip. Press the seams toward the bright pink strip. Make 18 strip sets using 36 tan strips and 18 bright pink strips.

   Use a ruler and rotary cutter to clean-cut the edges of the strip set. Crosscut the strips every 2" to make 162 segments.

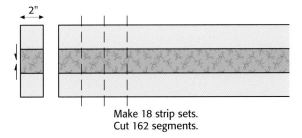

Make 18 strip sets.
Cut 162 segments.

3. Join 2 segments from step 1 and 1 segment from step 2 to complete a Nine Patch block. Make a total of 162 blocks.

Make 162.

Assembling the Quilt

1. Arrange the Nine Patch blocks and tan squares in rows. Using 6 pieced blocks and 10 plain blocks, sew 7 of row A as shown.

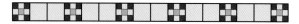

Row A
Make 7.

2. Using 10 pieced blocks and 6 plain blocks, sew 12 of row B as shown.

Row B
Make 6.

3. Referring to the quilt photo on page 18, sew the rows together, in an A-B-B order. Finish the quilt by adding one more row A to the bottom.

Adding the Borders

1. Sew the pink print strips together end to end to make 4 border strips. Trim the long border strips to fit your quilt top. Sew 2" x 86" inner border strips to opposite sides of the quilt. Sew 2" x 75½" inner border strips to the top and bottom of the quilt.
2. Sew the 8½" x 89" floral outer border strips to opposite sides of the quilt. Sew the 8½" x 91½" floral outer border strips to the top and bottom of the quilt.

Finishing

1. Mark the quilt top with a design of your choice.
2. Piece the backing horizontally to fit the quilt top.
3. Layer the quilt top with batting and backing; baste the layers together.
4. Hand or machine quilt as desired.
5. Trim the batting and backing even with the edges of the quilt top. Sew the dark brown print binding to the quilt.
6. Make a label and attach it to your quilt.

PILLOW TALK

If you want to have chocolates placed on your pillow, it certainly helps to start with lovely pillows! Make pillow shams to coordinate with your quilt by following the directions on page 115. You'll need 12 extra Nine Patch blocks and 12 extra tan squares for each sham. Sew them together as shown below. Add 2"-wide pink borders followed by 4½"-wide brown print borders.

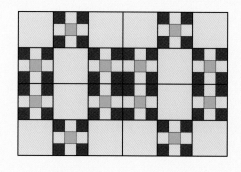

Favorite Hot Chocolate

INGREDIENTS

+ 4 cups (1 quart) milk
+ 6 (1.55-ounce) bars milk chocolate, broken into small pieces, or 1½ cups milk chocolate pieces
+ 1 teaspoon vanilla
+ Few drops of almond extract (optional)
+ Sweetened whipped cream (garnish)
+ Dark sweet chocolate shavings (garnish)

DIRECTIONS

1. In a large saucepan, combine 1 cup of the milk and all of the milk chocolate. Cook over medium-low heat, stirring frequently, until chocolate is melted. Gradually stir in the remaining 3 cups of milk. Cook and stir until milk is very hot, almost boiling, but do not boil.
2. Remove from heat. Stir in vanilla and, if desired, almond extract. Pour hot chocolate into mugs. Serve hot and garnish with sweetened whipped cream and chocolate shavings. Makes about six 6-ounce servings.

FLAVOR VARIATIONS

Omit almond extract and add one of the following with vanilla:

MINT HOT CHOCOLATE: ½ teaspoon mint extract OR ½ teaspoon peppermint extract OR 2 tablespoons crushed hard peppermint candy OR peppermint schnapps (to taste) OR 6 (1½") peppermint patties

VIENNESE HOT CHOCOLATE: ½ to ¾ teaspoon ground cinnamon and ¼ ground nutmeg

SWISS HOT MOCHA: 1 tablespoon instant coffee crystals OR coffee liqueur (to taste)

ORANGE HOT CHOCOLATE: ½ teaspoon orange extract OR 2 tablespoons orange liqueur

Starry Night

Did you ever stand out in the country—far away from streetlights or city lights—and look up at the night sky? The sky is illuminated as the galaxies glow in the darkness. The stars are amazing as they fill the heavens, and their constellations even create pictures in the sky.

In this quilt, gold stars twinkle on a bright blue traditional Log Cabin quilt to brighten any night in a country cottage. Make the blocks from scrappy light blue and dark blue strips; then appliqué bright gold stars on the patchwork.

May your guests find comfort under this quilt just as we find peace in stars glittering in the night sky. After a good night's sleep under this celestial design, wake your guests with the aroma of Oven-Baked French Toast cooking for breakfast.

Starry Night

Designed and appliquéd by Mimi Dietrich. Pieced by Mimi Dietrich and Emily Watson, Baltimore, Maryland, 2002.
Machine quilted by Linda Newsom, Crofton, Maryland.

Finished Quilt Size: 90½" x 90½"
Finished Block Size: 12" x 12"

Materials

Yardage is based on 42"-wide fabric unless otherwise stated.

4 yds. total of assorted bright blue prints for blocks

3¼ yds. dark blue print for outer border and binding★

3 yds. total of assorted light blue prints for blocks

1¼ yds. gold print for appliquéd stars and inner
border

8½ yds. fabric for backing

95" x 95" piece of batting

★Add 2½ yards to make pillowcases.

Cutting

*All measurements include ¼"-wide seam allowances. The
pattern for the appliqué stars is on page 26.*

From the assorted light blue prints, cut:
- 40 strips, 2" x 42"; from these strips, cut 36 pieces
  of *each* of the following lengths: 3½", 5", 6½", 8",
  9½", 11"

From the assorted bright blue prints, cut:
- 3 strips, 3½" x 42"; crosscut into 36 squares,
  3½" x 3½"
- 49 strips, 2" x 42"; from these strips, cut 36 pieces
  of *each* of the following lengths: 5", 6½", 8", 9½",
  11", 12½"

From the dark blue print, cut on the lengthwise grain:
- 2 strips, 8" x 75½"★
- 2 strips, 8" x 90½"★

From the remaining dark blue print, cut on the crosswise grain:
- 10 binding strips, 2" x 42"

From the gold print, cut:
  8 strips, 2" x 42"
  36 stars

Making the Log Cabin Blocks

You need 36 Log Cabin blocks for this quilt.

1. Sew a light blue 2" x 3½" strip to a bright blue
   square.

2. Turn the unit from step 1 a quarter turn to the left
   (counterclockwise) and add a light blue 2" x 5"
   strip to it.

3. Now turn the unit another quarter turn and add a
   bright blue 2" x 5" strip.

4. Turn the unit again and add a bright blue
   2" x 6½" strip. You've completed one round of
   logs.

5. Continue adding the light blue and bright blue
   strips to the block in the same fashion until you've
   made a total of 3 complete rounds to finish the
   block. Repeat all steps to make a total of 36 Log
   Cabin blocks.

   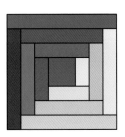

   Make 36.

Appliquéing the Stars

Appliqué a star on the bright blue side of 32 of the Log Cabin blocks.

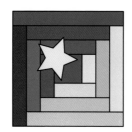

Assembling the Quilt

1. Referring to the quilt photograph on page 24, arrange the blocks as shown.
2. Sew the blocks together in rows; then sew the rows together.
3. Refer to the photo and appliqué the 4 remaining stars at the top, bottom, and 2 side corners of the center diamond motif created when the blocks were assembled.
4. Sew the gold strips together in pairs to make 4 inner border strips. Sew 2" x 72½" inner border strips to opposite sides of the quilt. Sew 2" x 75½" inner border strips to the top and bottom of the quilt.
5. Sew the 8" x 75½" dark blue outer border strips to opposite sides of the quilt. Sew the 8" x 90½" dark blue outer border strips to the top and bottom of the quilt.

Finishing

1. Mark the quilt top with a design of your choice.
2. Piece the backing vertically to fit the quilt top.
3. Layer the quilt top with batting and backing; baste the layers together.
4. Hand or machine quilt as desired.
5. Trim the batting and backing even with the edges of the quilt top. Sew the dark blue binding to the quilt.
6. Make a label and attach it to your quilt.

PILLOW TALK

Complete the heavenly decor with a pair of dark blue pillowcases and a tailored throw pillow. Follow the directions on page 115 to make the pillowcases. Make an extra Log Cabin block for the top of the throw pillow. Directions for completing a throw pillow are on pages 115–16. For a nice finishing touch, cover ½"-diameter cording with leftover gold fabric to trim the edges of the pillow.

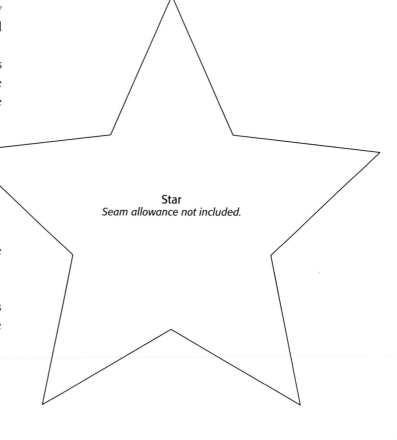

Star
Seam allowance not included.

Oven-Baked French Toast

INGREDIENTS

- 8 slices 1"-thick firm-textured French bread
- 8 eggs, slightly beaten
- 3½ cups milk
- 2 tablespoons granulated sugar
- 2 teaspoons vanilla
- 1 teaspoon ground cinnamon
- 1 cup firmly packed brown sugar
- ½ cup (1 stick) butter, at room temperature
- 2 tablespoons dark-colored corn syrup
- 1 cup coarsely chopped pecans or walnuts
- Sifted powdered sugar (optional)
- Maple syrup
- Assorted fresh fruit (garnish)

DIRECTIONS

1. Lightly butter a 13" x 9" x 2" baking dish. Arrange bread slices in a single layer in the prepared pan; set aside.

2. In a large mixing bowl, beat together eggs, milk, granulated sugar, vanilla, and cinnamon. Pour egg mixture evenly over the slices. Cover and chill in the refrigerator 6 to 24 hours.

3. Preheat the oven to 325°F (165°C).

4. For topping, in a medium-size mixing bowl, combine brown sugar, butter, and corn syrup. Stir in nuts. Evenly spoon nut mixture in small mounds over egg and bread mixture. Bake, uncovered, 55 to 60 minutes or until golden brown. Let stand 10 minutes.

5. If desired, sift powdered sugar over toast. Serve with warm maple syrup and fresh fruit. Makes 8 servings.

Spring Daydreams

One of my favorite flowers is the dogwood. It appears in early spring and signals the coming of warm weather, beautiful flowers, and bright colors in nature. It makes me take a break from my busy life, appreciate spring's message of renewal, and daydream!

I think of longer days, rays of sunshine, walks in warm weather, and bright quilts to make. What better place to daydream than under this inspirational quilt! The combination of patchwork and appliqué inspires any quilter to choose fabrics, get to the sewing machine, and start a beautiful new quilt.

Or maybe it would be just as nice to stay in bed under a lovely quilt and dream . . .

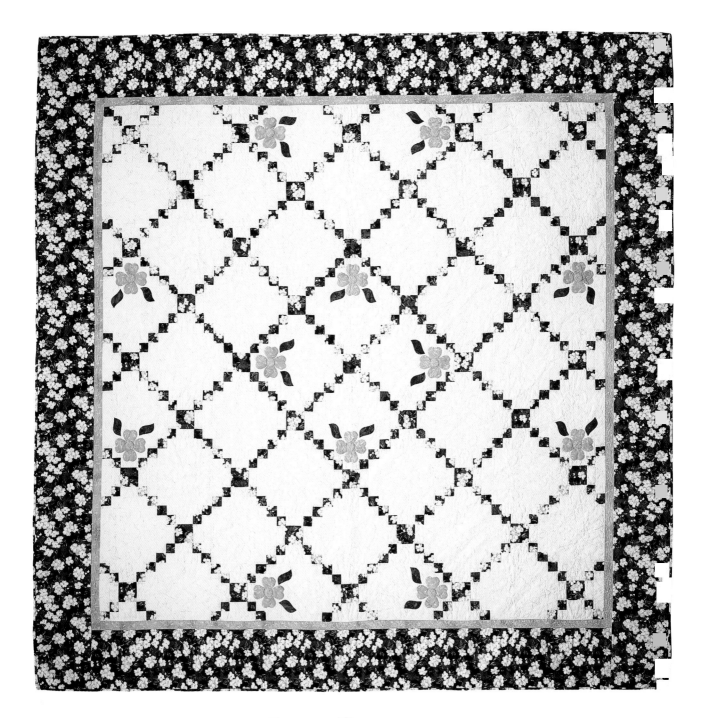

Spring Daydreams

Designed and appliquéd by Mimi Dietrich. Pieced by Mimi Dietrich and Emily Watson, Baltimore, Maryland, 2002.
Quilted by Amish friends.

Finished Quilt Size: 102½" x 102½"
Finished Block Size: 9" x 9"

Materials

Yardage is based on 42"-wide fabric unless otherwise stated.

6 yds. light pink print for patchwork blocks and
setting blocks

5½ yds. green floral print for patchwork blocks,
outer border, and binding★

1 yd. pink print for appliquéd flowers and inner
border

¼ yd. dark green print for appliquéd leaves

⅛ yd. or scraps of gold print for appliquéd flower
centers

9½ yds. fabric for backing

107" x 107" piece of batting

★Add 2½ yds. to make pillowcases.

Cutting

*All measurements include ¼"-wide seam allowances. Patterns
for the petals, leaf, and flower center are on page 34.*

From the light pink print, cut:
- 40 squares, 9½" x 9½"
- 8 strips, 2" x 42"
- 5 strips, 3½" x 42"
- 5 strips, 6½" x 42"; crosscut the strips to make 82
  rectangles, 2" x 6½"
- 5 strips, 6½" x 42"

From the green floral, cut on the lengthwise grain:
- 2 strips, 9½" x 84½"
- 2 strips, 9½" x 102½"

From the remaining green floral, cut:
- 4 strips, 3½" x 42"
- 20 strips, 2" x 42"
- 11 binding strips, 2" x 42"

From the pink print, cut:
- 9 strips, 2" x 42"
- 48 petals

From the dark green print, cut:
- 24 leaves

From the gold print, cut:
- 12 flower centers

Making the Single Irish Chain Blocks

You need 41 Single Irish Chain blocks for this quilt.

1. Sew a 2"-wide light pink print strip to each long
   edge of a 3½"-wide green floral strip. Press the
   seams toward the green strips. Make 4 strip sets.

   Use a ruler and rotary cutter to clean-cut the
   edges of the strip sets. Crosscut the strips into 41
   segments, 3½" wide.

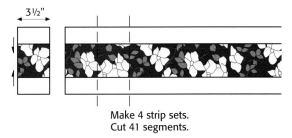

   Make 4 strip sets.
   Cut 41 segments.

2. Sew a 2"-wide green floral strip to each long edge
   of a 3½"-wide light pink print strip. Press the
   seams toward the green strips. Make 5 strip sets.

   Use a ruler and rotary cutter to clean-cut the
   edges of the strip sets. Crosscut the strips into 82
   segments, 2" wide.

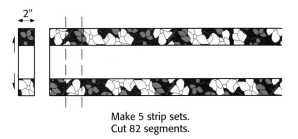

   Make 5 strip sets.
   Cut 82 segments.

3. Join 1 segment from step 1 and 2 segments from
   step 2 as shown. Make a total of 41 blocks.

   Make 41.

4. Sew a 2" x 6½" light pink rectangle to opposite sides of each block. Press the seams toward the pink rectangles.

 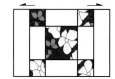

5. Sew a 2"-wide green floral strip to each long edge of a 6½"-wide light pink print strip. Press the seams toward the light pink print strips. Make 5 strip sets.

   Use a ruler and rotary cutter to clean-cut the edges of the strip sets. Crosscut the strips into 82 segments, 2" wide.

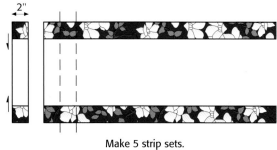

Make 5 strip sets.
Cut 82 segments.

6. Sew segments from step 5 to the remaining sides of the blocks to complete 41 Single Irish Chain blocks.

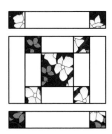 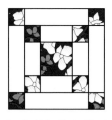

Single Irish Chain Block
Make 41.

Appliquéing the Flowers

1. For ease in appliquéing, sew 8 light pink squares and 8 patchwork blocks together as shown. Refer to the illustration to position the appliqué flowers and leaves. Make 4 of these units. Use your favorite appliqué technique to appliqué the heart-shaped petals, flower centers, and leaves to the quilt top.

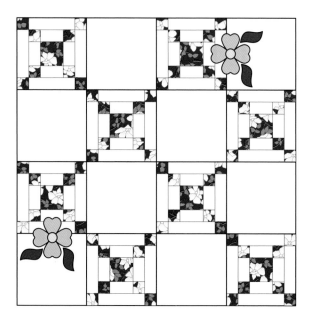

2. Sew 2 plain and 2 patchwork blocks together as shown. Appliqué flowers and leaves. Make 4 of these strips.

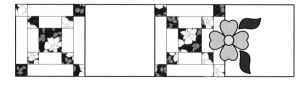

3. You will have a patchwork block left over; save it for the center of the quilt.

Assembling the Quilt

1. Arrange the pieced units as shown.

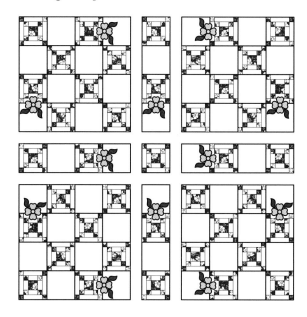

2. Sew the units together in rows; then sew the rows together.

3. Sew the 2"-wide pink strips together and trim to make 4 border strips. Trim the long strips to fit your quilt top. Sew 2" x 81½" inner border strips to opposite sides of the quilt. Sew 2" x 84½" inner border strips to the top and bottom of the quilt.

4. Sew the 9½" x 84½" green floral outer border strips to opposite sides of the quilt. Sew the 9½" x 102½" green floral outer border strips to the top and bottom of the quilt.

Finishing

1. Mark the quilt top with a design of your choice.
2. Piece the backing vertically to fit the quilt top.
3. Layer the quilt top with batting and backing; baste the layers together.
4. Hand or machine quilt as desired.
5. Trim the batting and backing even with the edges of the quilt top. Sew the green floral binding strips to the quilt.
6. Make a label and attach it to your quilt.

PILLOW TALK

To complete your new bedroom ensemble, make pillowcases using the directions on page 115. Make a throw pillow using the directions on pages 115–16. For the pillow top, appliqué a dogwood blossom and 4 leaves on a 9½" square of light pink background fabric. Frame the block with 2"-wide green floral borders. Add 3½"-wide pink print borders to finish the pillow.

Flower
Center

Petal

Seam allowances
not included.

Leaf

New Potatoes and Asparagus Frittata

INGREDIENTS

- 1 cup water
- 4 or 5 (4 ounces) tiny new potatoes, cut into small wedges (about 1 cup)
- 4 ounces fresh asparagus spears, cut into 1" lengths
- 6 eggs, slightly beaten
- ¼ cup milk
- 2 tablespoons snipped fresh parsley
- 1 teaspoon Italian seasoning, crushed
- ¼ teaspoon salt
- ¼ teaspoon crushed red pepper
- 1 tablespoon butter
- ½ cup (2 ounces) shredded Parmesan cheese
- Red or yellow tomatoes, cut into wedges

DIRECTIONS

1. In a medium-size saucepan, bring lightly salted water to a boil. Add potatoes. Reduce heat, cover, and simmer 6 minutes.

2. Add asparagus to potatoes and return to a boil. Reduce heat, cover, and simmer 2 to 3 minutes more or until vegetables are just tender. Drain vegetables well; set aside.

3. In a medium-size bowl, combine eggs, milk, parsley, Italian seasoning, salt, and red pepper; set aside. Preheat the broiler.

4. In a 10" broiler-proof skillet, melt butter over medium heat. Add potatoes and asparagus. Cook for 1 minute, stirring frequently. Pour egg mixture over vegetable mixture. Cook over medium-low heat, without stirring, until mixture begins to set on the bottom and around edge. Using a spatula or a large spoon, lift and fold partially cooked eggs so uncooked portion flows underneath. Continue cooking over medium heat 2 to 3 minutes or until eggs are cooked through, but still glossy and moist. Remove from heat. Sprinkle with Parmesan cheese.

5. Place broiler-proof skillet under the broiler. Broil 4" to 5" from the heat 1 to 2 minutes or until the top is just set. Cut into wedges. Serve with tomatoes. Makes 4 to 6 servings.

Friendship Baskets

Quilters love baskets! Country baskets are a favorite design used in many quilts. They remind us of the abundance we have and experiences and adventures that fill our lives.

As you appliqué a heart in each patchwork basket, think of a friend or family member who holds a special place in your heart. May your friendship baskets be full of love!

Show your guests they are special by adding a different twist to a favorite recipe. Serve Country Breakfast Pizza for a fun and easy start to the day.

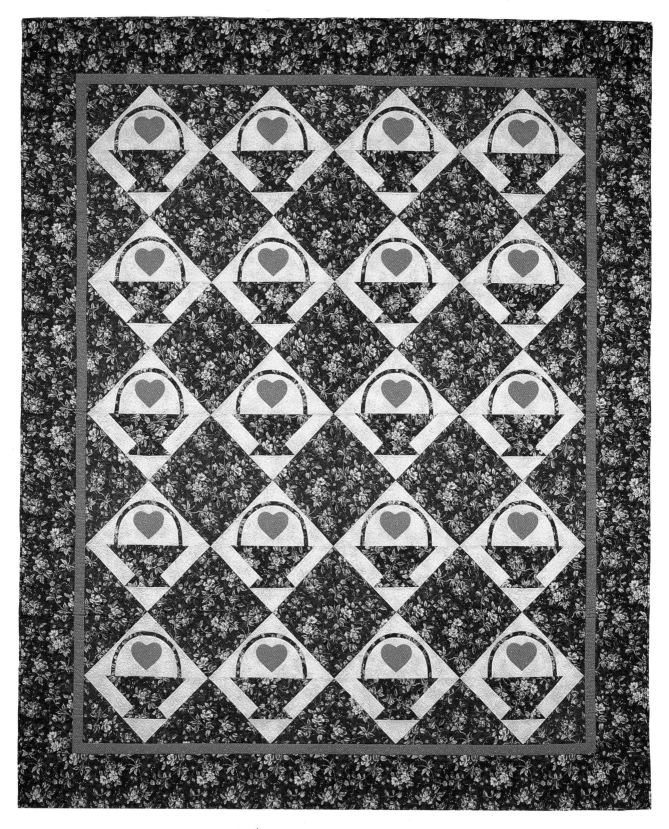

Friendship Baskets

By Mimi Dietrich, Baltimore, Maryland, 2002.
Machine quilted by Linda Newsom, Crofton, Maryland.

Finished Quilt Size: 85½" x 102½"
Finished Block Size: 12" x 12"

Materials

Yardage is based on 42"-wide fabric unless otherwise stated.

7 yds. blue floral for blocks, setting squares, setting triangles, outer border, and binding

2¾ yds. tan print for blocks★

1 yd. pink print for heart appliqués and inner border

8 yds. for backing

90" x 107" piece of batting

Gluestick

★Add 2½ yards for pillowcases.

Cutting

All measurements include ¼"-wide seam allowances. Pattern for the appliqué heart is on page 42.

From the blue floral, cut on the lengthwise grain:
- 2 strips, 7½" x 88½"
- 2 strips, 7½" x 85½"

From the remaining blue floral, cut:
- 12 squares, 12½" x 12½"
- 4 squares, 18¼" x 18¼"; cut each square twice diagonally to make 16 side setting triangles (2 will be extra)
- 2 squares, 9⅜" x 9⅜"; cut each square once diagonally to make 4 corner triangles
- 10 squares, 8⅞" x 8⅞"
- 20 squares, 2⅞" x 2⅞"
- 20 bias strips, 1" x 15"
- 10 binding strips, 2" x 42"

From the tan print, cut:
- 10 squares, 12⅞" x 12⅞"; cut each square once diagonally to make 20 triangles
- 10 squares, 4⅞" x 4⅞"; cut each square once diagonally to make 20 triangles
- 40 rectangles, 2½" x 8½"

From the pink print, cut:
- 9 strips, 2" x 42"
- 20 hearts

Making the Basket Blocks

You need 20 Basket blocks for this quilt.

1. Cut the 2⅞" blue floral squares in half diagonally to make 40 triangles. Sew a blue triangle to a tan print rectangle as shown to make the left side of the basket. Then draw a diagonal line at the opposite, square end of the rectangle as shown. Carefully cut off the triangle to make the left side of the basket. Make 20.

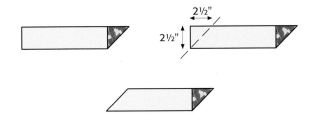

2. Sew the remaining 2⅞" blue floral triangles to the remaining tan print rectangles as shown. Trim the square ends to make the right side of the baskets. Make 20.

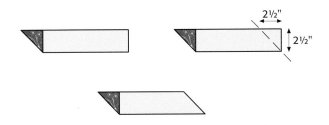

3. Cut the 8⅞" blue floral squares in half diagonally to make 20 basket triangles. Sew the units from step 1 to the left side of the blue triangles as shown.

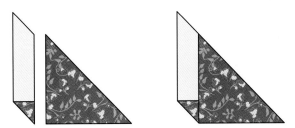

4. Sew the units from step 2 to the right sides of the blue triangles.

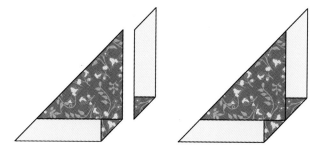

5. Sew the 4⅞" tan triangles to the bottom of the baskets as shown.

6. Using the placement guide on page 42, trace the handle lines and heart on the 12⅞" tan triangles.

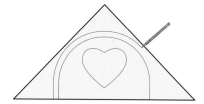

7. Fold the long edges of the 1"-wide blue floral bias strip into the center of the strips, wrong sides together, so that the raw edges meet. Baste along both edges of the handles with small stitches. Gently pull on one of the basting threads to ease each bias strip into a curved handle shape.

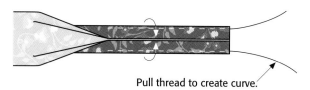

Pull thread to create curve.

8. Apply gluestick between the handle lines on a tan triangle. Place a blue handle between the lines, shaping the strip to fit the curve. Appliqué the handle. Repeat for all 20 triangles.

9. Appliqué the hearts using your favorite technique.

10. Sew the basket halves together to complete 20 blocks.

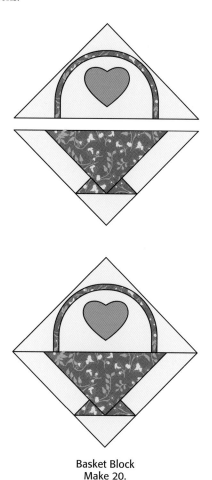

Basket Block
Make 20.

Assembling the Quilt

1. Arrange the basket blocks, 12½" setting squares, 18¼" setting triangles, and 9⅜" corner triangles as shown.

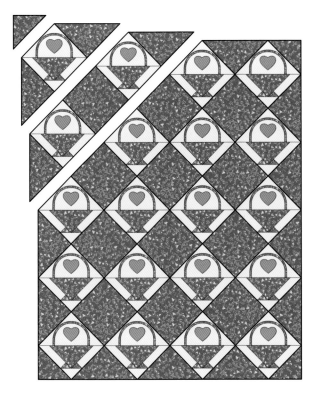

2. Sew the blocks, squares, and triangles together in diagonal rows; then sew the rows together.
3. Sew the pink print strips together to make 4 border strips. Trim the long strips to fit your quilt top. Sew 2" x 85½" pink print border strips to opposite sides of the quilt. Sew 2" x 71½" pink print border strips to the top and bottom of the quilt.
4. Sew 7½" x 88½" blue floral border strips to opposite sides of the quilt. Sew 7½" x 85½" blue floral border strips to the top and bottom of the quilt.

Finishing

1. Mark the quilt top with a design of your choice.
2. Piece the backing horizontally to fit the quilt top.
3. Layer the quilt top with batting and backing; baste the layers together.
4. Hand or machine quilt as desired.
5. Trim the batting and backing even with the edges of the quilt top. Sew the blue floral binding strips to the quilt.
6. Make a label and attach it to your quilt.

PILLOW TALK

Make coordinating pillowcases for your Friendship Baskets quilt using the directions on page 115. Toss in a throw pillow, too, following the directions on pages 115–16. Use a Basket block as the center; then add 3½"-wide blue floral borders to frame the pillow.

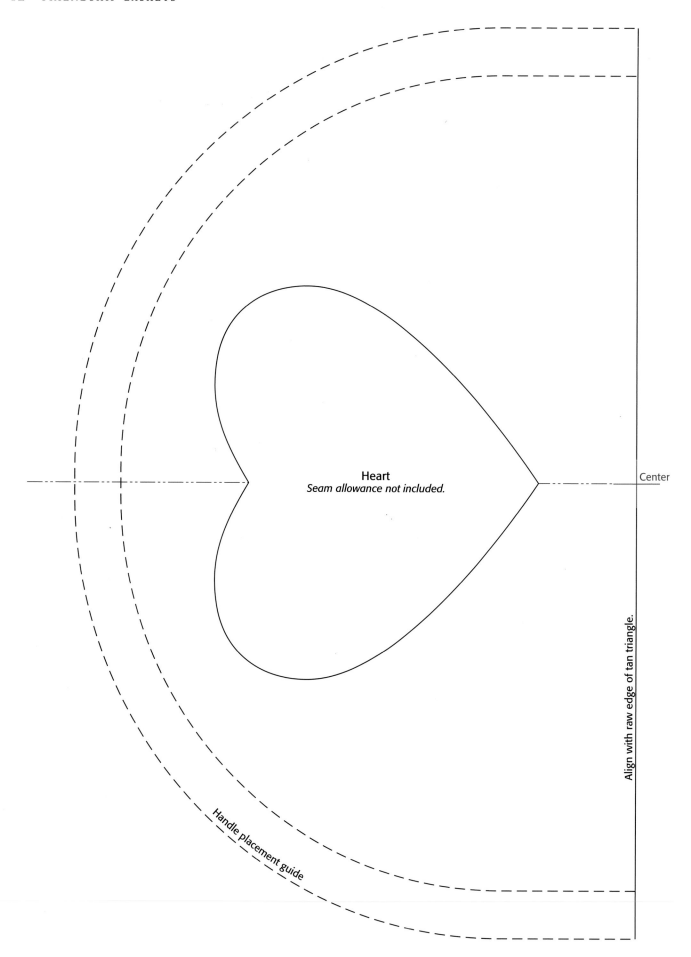

Heart
Seam allowance not included.

Center

Align with raw edge of tan triangle.

Handle placement guide

Country Breakfast Pizza

INGREDIENTS

- 8 eggs, slightly beaten
- ½ cup milk, half-and-half, or light cream
- ¼ teaspoon salt
- ¼ teaspoon ground black pepper
- ¼ teaspoon dried oregano, crushed
- 1 (14-ounce) Italian bread shell (such as Boboli)
- 2 tablespoons butter
- 1 cup sliced fresh mushrooms
- ½ cup chopped red or yellow onion
- ½ cup chopped red, yellow, and/or green bell pepper
- ½ cup chopped fully cooked ham or Canadian bacon
- 1 cup (4 ounces) shredded mozzarella cheese

DIRECTIONS

1. Preheat the oven to 375°F (190°C).
2. In a bowl, combine eggs, milk, salt, black pepper, and oregano; set aside. Place the bread shell on a large baking sheet or a 12" pizza pan.
3. In a large skillet, melt 1 tablespoon of the butter over medium heat. Add mushrooms, onion, bell pepper, and cook, stirring frequently, 5 minutes or until vegetables are tender. Remove vegetables and drain well. Stir in ham; set aside.
4. In the same skillet, melt the remaining 1 tablespoon butter over medium heat. Pour in egg mixture. Cook over medium heat, without stirring, until mixture begins to set on the bottom and around edge. Using a spatula or a large spoon, lift and fold partially cooked eggs so uncooked portion flows underneath. Continue cooking over medium heat 2 to 3 minutes or until eggs are cooked through, but still glossy and moist. Remove from heat.
5. To assemble pizza, sprinkle half of the cheese over bread shell. Top with cooked eggs, vegetable mixture, and remaining cheese. Bake 8 to 10 minutes or until cheese is melted. Cut into wedges to serve. Makes 6 servings.

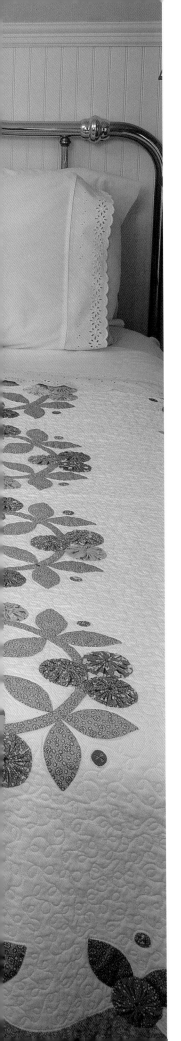

Garden Comfort

Do you remember visits to your grandmother's house? Do they call to mind times past when life was simpler? Let your imagination smell the cinnamon buns baking, chocolate chip cookies warm from the oven, and cocoa made from scratch on the stove, not in a microwave.

The quilts were all traditional patterns and the fabrics were all printed with calico flowers, tiny geometric prints, and little animals. Many of our grandmothers made quilts using yo-yos—gathered circles of fabric that created a garden of dimensional flowers. The throw pillows shown on this bed are inspired by the traditional quilt pattern Grandmother's Flower Garden.

Just cuddle under this quilt and remember the good old days—or invite your grandmother over to visit and reminisce!

Garden Comfort

By Mimi Dietrich, Baltimore, Maryland, 2002.
Machine quilted by Linda Newsom, Crofton, Maryland.

Finished Quilt Size: 78½" x 94½"
Finished Block Size: 16" x 16"

Materials

Yardage is based on 42"-wide fabric unless otherwise stated.

7½ yds. white-on-white print for blocks★
16 fat quarters of assorted pink, lavender, blue, and
    yellow prints for appliquéd circles and yo-yos
3 yds. lavender print for border and binding★★
2 yds. green print for appliqués
5¾ yds. white fabric for backing
83" x 99" piece of batting
Freezer paper
★*Add 2½ yds. for pillowcases*
★★ *Add 1½ yds. for 3 throw pillows*

Note: You can cut 12 yo-yos from each fat quarter, but
a long quarter yard will yield only 8 yo-yos.

Cutting

*All measurements include ¼"-wide seam allowances. Patterns
for the appliqué leaf, small circle, and yo-yo flower are on
pages 52–53.*

From the white-on-white print, cut:
- 12 squares, 16½" x 16½"
- 14 rectangles, 15½" x 16½"
- 4 squares, 15½" x 15½"

From the green print, cut:
- 12 bias strips, 1" x 33"
- 144 leaves

From each of the assorted fat quarters, cut:
- 11 yo-yo circles★
- 5 small circles

From the lavender print, cut:
- 4 squares, 15½" x 15½"
- 14 rectangles, 7½" x 16½"
- 9 binding strips, 2" x 42"

★*You can make a plastic template from the pattern on page 53,
or simply use a music or computer CD as a template—they're
just the right size—and durable, too!*

Appliquéing the Blocks

1. Make 4 photocopies of the quarter-block wreath
   pattern on page 52. Tape the 4 patterns together
   to make a full-size wreath pattern.

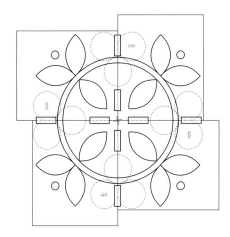

2. Center the design and trace the wreath onto the
   16½" white squares.
3. Fold the long edges of the green bias strips into
   the center of the strip, wrong sides together, so
   that the raw edges meet. Baste along both edges of
   each strip with small stitches. Gently pull on one
   of the basting threads to ease each bias strip into
   a curve.

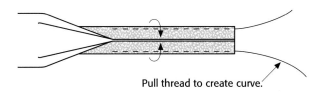

Pull thread to create curve.

4. Appliqué the bias strip wreath in place. Begin
   stitching under the yo-yo flower placement, folding under the short end of the wreath ¼" to
   finish the edges where they meet.

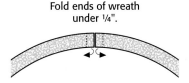

Fold ends of wreath
under ¼".

5. Appliqué the leaves and small circles using your favorite method. Repeat to make 12 blocks.

Appliquéing the Borders

The scalloped border is easy to assemble because it's made of individual blocks rather than long border strips. You need 14 side border pieces and 4 border corners.

1. Make a scallop border pattern by folding a 7½" x 16½" piece of freezer paper in half, shiny sides together, as shown. Place the fold of the paper on the fold line indicated on the pattern on page 53 and trace the scallop. Cut out the template along the traced line.

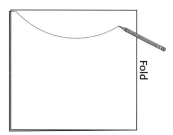

2. Unfold the freezer-paper template and place it on a lavender rectangle to mark and cut the scallops. You can press the paper in place to hold it while you trace along the curve. Peel it off and reuse to mark each of the lavender rectangles.

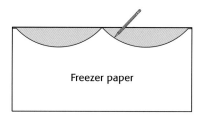

3. Place each lavender scallop piece on top of a white rectangle and appliqué the scalloped edges.

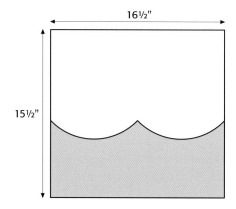

4. Trim the excess white fabric away from underneath the lavender fabric to reduce bulk in the block.

5. Appliqué 2 leaves and a small circle at the center point of each border scallop piece as shown.

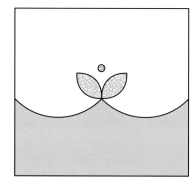

6. To make the corner pattern, trace a folded scallop border pattern as in step 1. Cut the paper in half along the fold. Place the 2 paper patterns in opposite corners of the lavender corner squares. Mark the curved line, cut out the scallop (do not cut along the straight fold lines), and appliqué the lavender fabric to a 15½" white corner square. Repeat to make 4 corners.

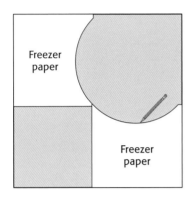

Making Yo-Yos

1. Make a plastic template from the yo-yo circle pattern on page 53, or use a CD as your template. Using a pencil, mark around the edge of your circle template on your fabric.
2. Cut out the circle exactly on the pencil line.
3. Turn under ¼" around the outside edge of the circle, folding wrong sides together.
4. Using a double thread about 20" long, sew a running stitch around the outside of the circle.

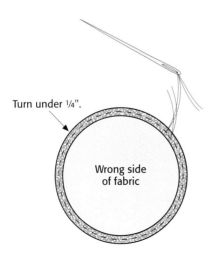

5. When you get all the way around the circle, take your last stitch next to the first one on the right side. Pull the threads to gather the edges together into the center of the circle.

6. Use the 2 threads to tie a knot. Pinch the gathers together and tie a few more knots to hold it tight. Thread the needle again and stitch the threads into the gathers of the yo-yo to hide the ends.
7. Appliqué the edges of the yo-yos to the wreaths and borders of your quilt.

TIPS FOR SUCCESSFUL YO-YOS

- Use heavy quilting thread.
- Do not tie a knot where you begin; leave a 4"-long tail of thread.
- While you stitch, hold the circle so that you are looking at the ¼" turned over the wrong side of the fabric.
- Take the first stitch from the right side of the fabric, up through the ¼" turned fabric.
- Sew close to the fold on the turned edge.
- To help the yo-yo close tightly, sew the running stitches "little on top" (the turned ¼" piece) and "big on the bottom" (the right side of the fabric). I like to remember this by thinking about body shapes!
- The little stitches should be about ⅛" long; the big stitches should be about ½" long.
- If you sew with very small running stitches, the finished yo-yo will have a big hole in the center.

Assembling the Quilt

1. Arrange the Wreath and border blocks as shown.

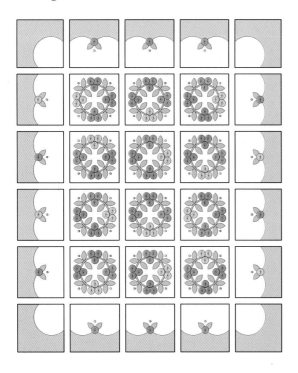

2. Sew the blocks together in rows; then sew the rows together to complete the quilt top.
3. Appliqué the remaining small circles, yo-yos, and leaves on the borders where the scallops meet.

Finishing the Quilt

1. Mark the quilt top with a design of your choice.
2. Piece the backing horizontally to fit the quilt top.
3. Layer the quilt top with batting and backing; baste the layers together.
4. Hand or machine quilt as desired.
5. Trim the batting and backing even with the edges of the quilt top. Sew the lavender print binding to the quilt.
6. Make and attach a label to your quilt.

PILLOW TALK

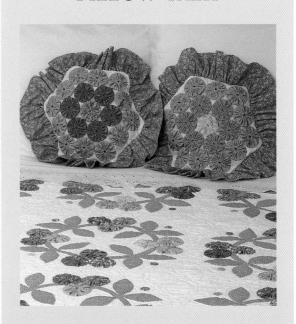

This romantic garden quilt looks oh-so pretty when combined with matching crisp white pillowcases and a yo-yo throw pillow or two on the bed. Make the pillowcases using the directions on page 115.

To make a throw pillow, appliqué a yo-yo in the center of a 12" square of white fabric. Sew 6 yo-yos around the center yo-yo to make a flower. Then add an outer ring of 12 green yo-yos to complete the design. Trim the white fabric so it is 1" larger than the flower all around; your pillow will be a hexagon shape.

For each throw pillow, cut 2 strips of lavender print, 7" x 42", for ruffles. Sew the strips together end to end to form a ring. Fold the strips in half lengthwise, wrong sides together. Gather the raw edges and sew to the edges of the white pillow-top fabric. Add the pillow back referring to the basic pillow instructions on pages 115–16 and turn right side out.

Butter-Almond Coffee Cake

INGREDIENTS

- ½ cup (1 stick) unsalted butter, at room temperature
- ½ cup sugar
- 2 tablespoons amaretto or fresh orange juice
- 1½ cups finely chopped almonds
- 2¾ cups all-purpose flour
- ¾ cup sugar
- ¾ cup (1½ sticks) unsalted butter, cold
- ½ cup sliced almonds
- ¾ teaspoon ground nutmeg
- ½ teaspoon baking powder
- ½ teaspoon baking soda
- ¼ teaspoon salt
- 1 egg, lightly beaten
- ¾ cup buttermilk
- Sifted powdered sugar (optional)
- Fresh raspberries or edible flowers (garnish)

DIRECTIONS

1. Preheat the oven to 350°F (175°C). Grease and flour an 11" tart pan with a removable bottom; set aside.

2. For filling, in a medium-size bowl, beat the ½ cup soft butter with an electric mixer at medium speed 30 seconds. Add the ½ cup sugar and amaretto. Beat well. Stir in almonds; set aside.

3. For cake, in a large bowl, stir together flour and the ¾ cup sugar. Using a pastry cutter or 2 knives, cut in the ¾ cup cold butter until the mixture resembles coarse crumbs. Measure ½ cup of the flour mixture for crumb topping. Place in a small bowl and stir in sliced almonds; set aside. Into the remaining flour mixture, stir nutmeg, baking powder, baking soda, and salt. Combine egg and buttermilk. Add egg mixture to flour mixture, stirring only until dry ingredients are just moistened.

4. Using a narrow metal spatula, spread two-thirds of the batter over the bottom and about 1" up the side of the prepared pan. Spread filling over batter. Spoon the remaining batter in small mounds on top. Sprinkle with the reserved crumb topping.

5. Bake 30 to 40 minutes or until a wooden pick inserted in the center comes out clean. Let stand in pan on a wire rack 15 minutes. Remove the side of the tart pan. Cut into wedges. If desired, sift powdered sugar over the tart. Garnish with fresh raspberries and edible flowers. Serve warm or at room temperature. Makes 8 to 10 servings.

RECIPE TIP: If you don't have buttermilk, substitute soured milk. To make ¾ cup soured milk, place 2 teaspoons lemon juice in a glass measuring cup. Add enough milk to measure ¾ cup. Stir and let stand at room temperature 5 minutes.

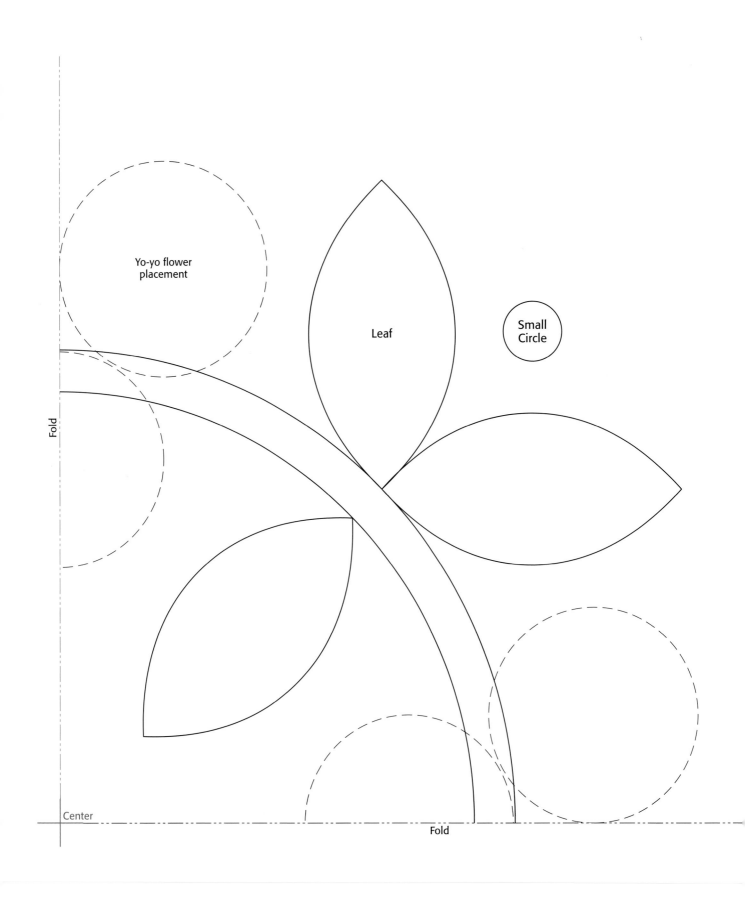

Yo-yo flower
placement

Leaf

Small
Circle

Fold

Center

Fold

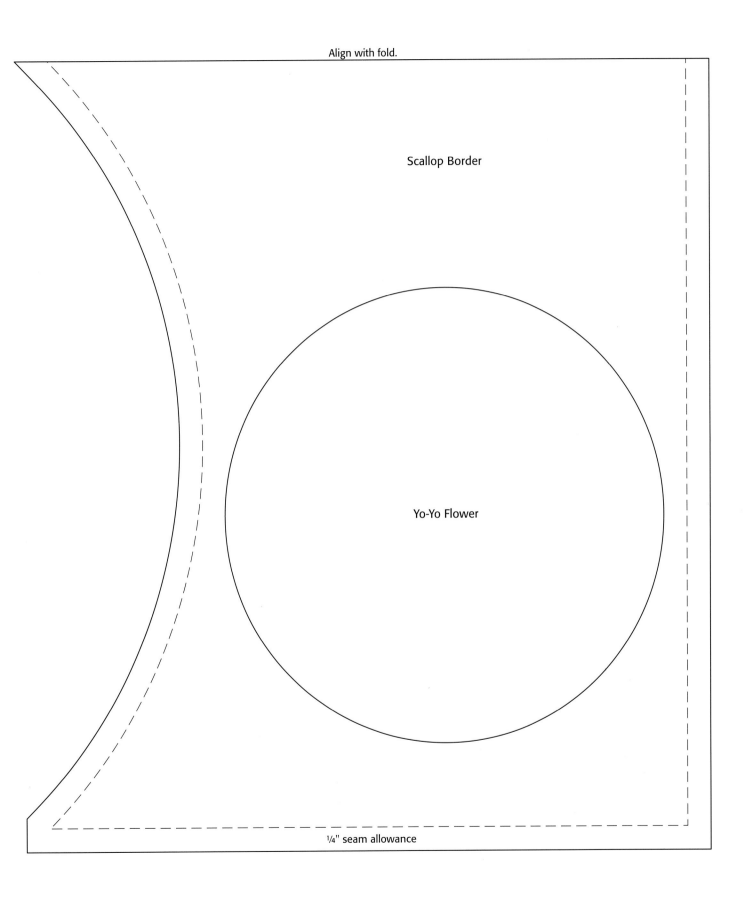

Align with fold.

Scallop Border

Yo-Yo Flower

¼" seam allowance

Honeymoon Suite

This quilt block has several names, but my favorite is Wedding Ring. It's easy to make and fun to position dark fabrics so that the squares and triangles form the ring in the center of the design. This quilt would be perfect to make for a wedding or anniversary celebration.

Using a striped border fabric adds an elegant finish to the quilt. It's easy to match the design in the mitered corners because the quilt is square; placing one of the border stripe patterns in the center of the quilt edge is the secret. Tone-on-tone fabrics matched with the colors in the stripe give the quilt a very coordinated look.

Honeymoon Suite

Designed by Mimi Dietrich. Pieced by Mimi Dietrich and Emily Watson, Baltimore, Maryland, 2002.
Machine quilted by Linda Newsom, Crofton, Maryland.

Finished Quilt Size: 93" x 93"
Finished Block Size: 15" x 15"

Materials

Yardage is based on 42"-wide fabric unless otherwise stated.

3 yds. dark purple print for blocks, sashing, and
　binding
3 yds. medium purple print for blocks and setting
　triangles*
2¾ yds. border print for border**
2 yds. light gray print for blocks
⅝ yd. fuchsia print for blocks and sashing squares
　and triangles
8½ yds. for backing
97" x 97" piece of batting

Add 2½ yards for pillowcases.
**Make sure your border print fabric has 4 stripes of the
design you want to use for your borders. You should also buy
one extra pattern repeat (¼ to ½ yard) to insure that the same
design will be placed in each mitered corner.*

Cutting

All measurements include ¼"-wide seam allowances.

From the dark purple print, cut:
- 3 strips, 3⅞" x 42"; crosscut into 26 squares,
  3⅞" x 3⅞"; cut each square once diagonally to
  make 52 triangles
- 36 strips, 3½" x 15½"
- 10 binding strips, 2" x 42"

From the light gray print, cut:
- 5 strips, 3½" x 42"
- 11 strips, 3⅞" x 42"; crosscut into 104 squares,
  3⅞" x 3⅞"; cut each square once diagonally to
  make 208 triangles

From the medium purple print, cut:
- 5 strips, 3½" x 42"
- 8 strips, 3⅞" x 42"; crosscut into 78 squares,
  3⅞" x 3⅞"; cut each square once diagonally to
  make 156 triangles

- 2 squares, 22½" x 22½"; cut each square twice
  diagonally to make 8 triangles
- 2 squares, 11½" x 11½"; cut each square once
  diagonally to make 4 triangles

From the fuchsia print, cut:
- 25 squares, 3½" x 3½"
- 3 squares, 5½" x 5½"; cut each square twice diagonally to make 12 triangles

**From the border print, cut on the lengthwise
grain:**
- 4 strips, 8½" x the length of your fabric (Refer to
  "Adding the Border" on page 58 before cutting.)

Making the Wedding
Ring Blocks

You need 13 Wedding Ring blocks for this quilt.

1. Sew a dark purple triangle to a light gray triangle.
   Press the seams toward the dark purple triangle.
   Make 52 of these units.

Make 52.

2. Sew a 3⅞" medium purple triangle to a light gray
   triangle. Press the seams toward the medium purple triangle. Make 156 of these units.

Make 156.

3. Sew 4 triangle squares together as shown. Make 52 of these units.

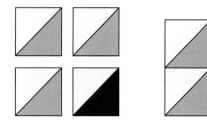

Make 52.

4. Sew a medium purple strip to a light gray strip. Repeat to make 5 strip sets. Crosscut the strip sets into 52 segments, 3½" wide.

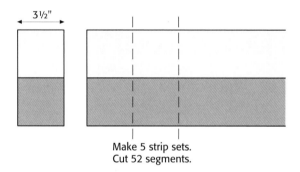

Make 5 strip sets.
Cut 52 segments.

5. Arrange the units as shown. Use a fuchsia print square in the center. Sew the units into rows; then sew the rows together to make a Wedding Ring block. Repeat to make a total of 13 blocks.

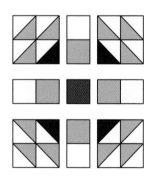
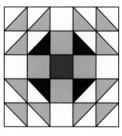

Make 13.

Assembling the Quilt

Arrange the Wedding Ring blocks, the dark purple 3½" x 15½" sashing strips, and the fuchsia sashing squares and triangles as shown. Sew dark purple sashing strips to the blocks to make diagonal rows. Add medium purple 11½" setting triangles to the ends of the rows. Sew the remaining dark purple sashing strips and fuchsia sashing squares and triangles to make diagonal rows. Sew the rows together.

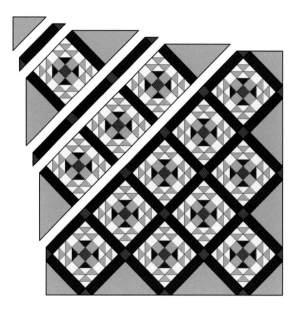

Adding the Border

1. Fold a border strip in half, arranging the design so that the middle of a symmetrical motif is centered on the fold. Place a pin at fold mark. This is now the center of your border.

Pin

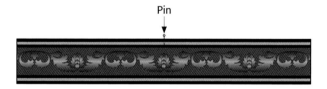

2. Match the center of the border to the center of the quilt edge. Carefully pin the border to the quilt, making sure that identical designs fall at the quilt corners. Sew the border to the quilt edge, stopping ¼" from each end.
3. Repeat steps 1 and 2 for the remaining 3 borders, making sure the same edge of the border stripe is sewn to all 4 quilt edges.
4. Miter the border corners, referring to the directions on page 122.

Finishing

1. Mark the quilt top with a design of your choice.
2. Piece the backing vertically to fit the quilt top.
3. Layer the quilt top with batting and backing; baste the layers together.
4. Hand or machine quilt as desired.
5. Trim the batting and backing even with the edges of the quilt top. Sew the dark purple print binding to the quilt.
6. Make a label and attach it to your quilt.

PILLOW TALK

Using the medium purple print, make a pair of pillowcases using the directions on page 115. Make a coordinating throw pillow using the basic directions on pages 115–16. Use a Wedding Ring block as the center of the pillow top, and add 3½"-wide borders to frame the block.

Citrus Champagne Punch

INGREDIENTS

- 2 cups water
- ½ cup sugar
- ½ (12-ounce) can frozen lemonade concentrate, thawed
- ½ (12-ounce) can frozen limeade concentrate, thawed
- ½ (12-ounce) can frozen tangerine juice concentrate or orange juice concentrate, thawed
- 1 (750-milliliter) bottle of Champagne, chilled, or a 1-liter bottle of ginger ale, chilled
- 1 (750-milliliter) bottle of dry white wine, chilled, or a 1-liter bottle of carbonated water, chilled
- Fruited Ice (see below)

DIRECTIONS

1. In a large bowl, combine water and sugar. Stir until sugar dissolves. Stir in lemonade, limeade, and tangerine juice concentrates.
2. In a large punch bowl, gently combine lemonade mixture, Champagne, and wine. Remove the fruited ice from ring mold or ice-cube trays. Place in punch bowl. Makes about 2½ quarts (twenty 4-ounce servings).

FRUITED ICE: Fill a 6-cup ring mold or 4 ice-cube trays two-thirds full with water and freeze overnight. Arrange strawberry slices, blueberries, kiwifruit slices, and fresh mint leaves on top of ice. Fill mold or trays with water. Freeze until solid.

Count Your Blessings

A strippy quilt like this is a perfect setting to showcase a classic striped fabric and coordinating prints. The combination looks great on any bed. The basic beauty of the quilt comes from a gorgeous printed floral stripe. The patchwork flower blocks are made from strips that are easy to cut and even easier to sew.

As you sew the blocks into strips, count a blessing for each one, and smile! May your blessings bring your guests sweet dreams when they sleep under this special quilt.

Count Your Blessings

Designed by Mimi Dietrich. Pieced by members of the Helping Hands Quilt Guild: Kay Butler, Louise Brown, Sue Ellen Dennis, Anne Edwards, Flo Gomory, Debbie Hibbert, Janet Johnson, Cindy Mayan, Jennie Palmer, Pam Sullivan, Barb Shutz, Lauren Taylor, Joyce Wade; Dover, Delaware; 2002. Quilted by Rachel and Sarah Hershberger, Michigan.

Finished Quilt Size: 84¼" x 96⅛"
Finished Block Size: 4½" x 4½"
Diagonal Block Measurement: 6⅜"

Materials

Yardage is based on 42"-wide fabric.

6 yds. floral stripe (stripes printed approximately
    6½" wide)
2½ yds. light floral print for patchwork setting
    triangles
1¼ yds. light green print for patchwork
1 yd. dark green print for patchwork and binding
1 yd. dark rose print for patchwork
½ yd. rose print for patchwork
8 yds. fabric for backing
89" x 101" piece of batting

Cutting

All measurements include ¼"-wide seam allowances.

From the floral stripe, cut:
• 7 strips, 7" x 100"

Note: Cut the strips so that the floral designs are positioned the same on each strip. The strips are longer than the quilt measurement and will be trimmed to the correct size later.

From the rose print, cut:
• 5 strips, 2" x 42"

From the dark rose print, cut:
• 14 strips, 2" x 42"

From the light floral print, cut:
• 42 squares, 7⅝" x 7⅝"; cut each square twice
  diagonally to make 168 triangles
• 12 squares, 4⅛" x 4⅛"; cut each square once
  diagonally to make 24 triangles

From the light green print, cut:
• 9 strips, 2" x 42"
• 5 strips, 3½" x 42"

From the dark green print, cut:
5 strips, 2" x 42"
10 binding strips, 2" x 42"

Making the Patchwork Blocks

You need 90 blocks for this quilt.

1. Sew a rose strip to a dark rose strip. Press the seams toward the dark strips. Make 5 strip sets. Use a ruler and rotary cutter to clean-cut the edges of the strip set. Crosscut the strips into 2"-wide segments; cut 90 segments.

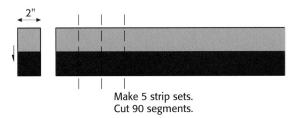

Make 5 strip sets.
Cut 90 segments.

2. Sew a dark rose strip to a 2"-wide light green strip. Press the seams toward the green strips. Make 9 strip sets. Use a ruler and rotary cutter to clean-cut the edges of the strip set. Crosscut the strips into 3½"-wide segments; cut 90 segments.

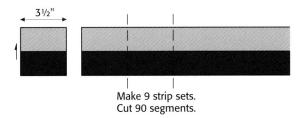

Make 9 strip sets.
Cut 90 segments.

3. Sew a segment from step 2 to each segment from step 1 as shown. Press the seams toward the dark rose rectangles.

4. Sew a 3½"-wide light green strip to a dark green print strip. Press the seams toward the light strips. Make 5 strip sets. Use a ruler and rotary cutter to clean-cut the edges of the strip sets. Crosscut the strips into 2"-wide segments; cut 90 segments.

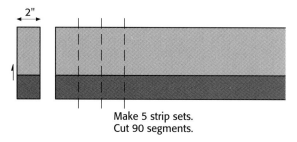

Make 5 strip sets.
Cut 90 segments.

5. Sew the green segments to the patchwork units as shown to make 90 squares.

Make 90.

Assembling the Quilt

1. Arrange the patchwork blocks and 7⅝" light floral side setting triangles as shown. Sew the blocks and triangles together in diagonal rows.

2. Join the rows, adding the 4⅛" light floral corner setting triangles last. Make 6 strips of 15 patchwork blocks each.

3. Measure the length of the 6 patchwork strips. Take the average length and trim the floral stripe strips to this measurement. Arrange the floral stripe strips and patchwork strips as shown and sew them together to complete the quilt top.

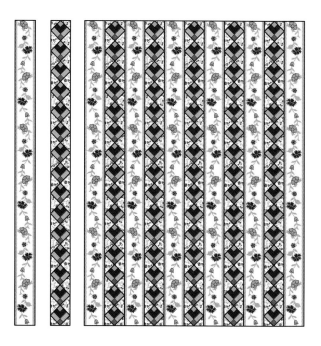

Finishing

1. Mark the quilt top with a design of your choice.
2. Piece the backing horizontally to fit the quilt top.
3. Layer the quilt top with batting and backing; baste the layers together.
4. Hand or machine quilt as desired.
5. Trim the batting and backing even with the edges of the quilt top. Sew the dark green print binding to the quilt.
6. Make a label and attach it to your quilt.

Oatmeal Crème Brûlée

INGREDIENTS

- 1⅔ cups old-fashioned oats
- 3 egg yolks
- ¼ cup granulated sugar
- 1 cup half-and-half or light cream
- ¾ teaspoon vanilla
- ½ cup snipped pitted dates, raisins, currants, golden raisins, or mixed dried fruit bits
- ¼ cup firmly packed brown sugar
- 1 teaspoon ground cinnamon
- ½ teaspoon salt
- 3 cups water
- Peeled peach slices, nectarines, or plums (optional)
- ⅓ cup firmly packed brown sugar

DIRECTIONS

1. Preheat the oven to 350°F (175°C).
2. In a shallow baking pan, evenly spread oats. Bake, stirring occasionally, 15 to 20 minutes or until oats are lightly browned; set aside.
3. For custard sauce, in a medium-size heavy saucepan, whisk egg yolks until thoroughly mixed. Whisk in granulated sugar, 1 tablespoon at a time. In a small saucepan, heat half-and-half over medium heat just until tiny bubbles form around the edge. Slowly stir hot half-and-half into egg yolk mixture. Cook over medium-low heat, stirring constantly with a wooden spoon, just until the mixture thickens enough to coat the wooden spoon. (The sauce should be thick enough to leave a smooth, creamy layer that clings to the surface of the wooden spoon.) Remove from heat. Stir in vanilla. Pour custard into a small bowl; set aside.
4. For oatmeal, in another small bowl, combine toasted oats, dates, the ¼ cup brown sugar, the cinnamon, and salt. In a medium-size saucepan, bring water to a boil over high heat. Gradually stir in oat mixture. Reduce heat and simmer, stirring often, 5 to 7 minutes or until thickened. Remove from heat. Cover; let stand 3 minutes.
5. Preheat the broiler. Place six ¾-cup (4") ramekins or 6-ounce custard cups on a large baking sheet.
6. Evenly divide oatmeal mixture among the dishes. Pour custard sauce over oatmeal. If desired, arrange peaches on top. Sprinkle with brown sugar. Broil 4" to 5" from heat, watching carefully and turning the cups as necessary, 1 to 2 minutes or until sugar turns golden brown and bubbly. Remove from oven. Let stand 2 minutes. Serve warm. Makes 6 servings.

Rise and Shine

Wouldn't it be great to wake up each morning in a room bathed in sunlight? Bring the outdoors inside when you choose sunny yellow and warm gold fabrics to make this quilt.

The star pattern in this quilt is a traditional design known as Evening Star, but this version will help you start your day on a bright note, ready to rise and shine! This fabric combination is especially wonderful in the fall, helping summer colors linger into autumn. As a special treat, wake your guests with the spicy aroma of Streusel-Topped Pumpkin Muffins.

Rise and Shine

Designed by Mimi Dietrich. Pieced by Mimi Dietrich and Emily Watson, Baltimore, Maryland, 2002.
Machine quilted by Linda Newsom, Crofton, Maryland.

Finished Quilt Size: 82¼" x 103½"
Finished Block Size: 12" x 12"

Materials

Yardage is based on 42"-wide fabric.

5 yds. dark gold print for blocks, sashing squares, triangles, outer border, and binding
5 yds. medium gold print for blocks, setting strips, and inner border
3¼ yds. yellow print for blocks and setting triangles*
7¾ yds. for backing
86" x 108" piece of batting
Add 2½ yards to make pillowcases.

Cutting

All measurements include ¼"-wide seam allowances.

From the yellow print, cut:
- 19 strips, 3½" x 42"; from the strips, cut:
  - 72 squares, 3½" x 3½"
  - 72 rectangles, 3½" x 6½"
- 3 squares, 8¼" x 8¼"; cut each square twice diagonally to make 12 setting triangles. (There will be 2 extra.)
- 2 squares, 9⅜" x 9⅜"; cut each square once diagonally to make 4 corner setting triangles

From the medium gold print, cut on the lengthwise grain:
- 2 border strips, 3½" x 85½"
- 2 border strips, 3½" x 70¼"

From the remaining medium gold print, cut on the crosswise grain:
- 3 strips, 6½" x 42"; cut strips into 18 squares, 6½" x 6½"
- 16 strips, 3½" x 42"; cut strips into 48 sashing strips, 3½" x 12½"

From the dark gold print, cut on the lengthwise grain:
- 2 border strips, 6½" x 91½"
- 2 border strips, 6½" x 82¼"

From the remaining dark gold print, cut on the crosswise grain:
- 15 strips, 3½" x 42"; cut the strips into 161 squares, 3½" x 3½"
- 7 squares, 3⅞" x 3⅞"; cut squares in half once diagonally to make 14 triangles
- 10 binding strips, 2" x 42"

Making the Evening Star Blocks

You need 18 Evening Star blocks for this quilt.

1. Using a pencil, draw a diagonal line on the wrong side of the 3½" dark gold square. Mark 144 squares.
2. With right sides together, place a dark gold square on half of a yellow rectangle as shown. Sew on the line; then trim away the bottom 2 layers, leaving a ¼" seam allowance. Press the dark gold fabric over the stitched line to create a triangle.

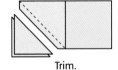

Stitch.   Trim.

Press.

3. Place a dark gold square on the other end of the rectangle as shown. Sew on the line, trim, and press. Repeat to make 72 units.

4. Sew a pieced unit to opposite sides of a 6½" medium gold square as shown. Repeat to make 18 of these block centers.

  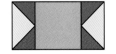

5. Sew yellow squares to opposite ends of a pieced unit as shown. Repeat to make 36 of these star point units.

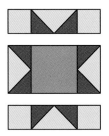 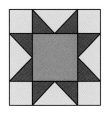

6. Sew the units together to make an Evening Star block. Repeat to make 18 blocks.

Make 18.

Assembling the Quilt

Arrange the patchwork blocks, 3½" x 12½" medium gold sashing strips, and dark gold sashing squares and triangles as shown. Sew medium gold sashing strips to the blocks to make diagonal rows. Add 18¼" yellow setting triangles to the ends of the rows. Sew medium gold sashing strips, dark gold sashing squares, and dark gold triangles together to make the diagonal sashing rows. Sew the rows together, referring to the quilt photograph on page 68 and the assembly diagram below.

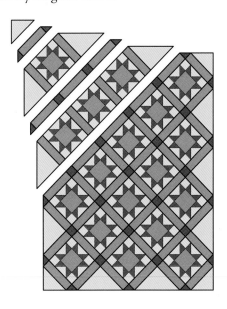

Adding the Borders

1. Sew the 3½" x 85½" medium gold strips to opposite sides of the quilt. Sew the 3½" x 70¼" medium gold strips to the top and bottom of the quilt. Press all seams toward the borders.
2. Sew the 6½" x 91½" dark gold strips to opposite sides of the quilt. Sew the 6½" x 82¼" dark gold strips to the top and bottom of the quilt.

Finishing

1. Mark the quilt top with a design of your choice.
2. Piece the backing horizontally to fit the quilt top.
3. Layer the quilt top with batting and backing; baste the layers together.
4. Hand or machine quilt as desired.
5. Trim the batting and backing even with the edges of the quilt top. Sew the gold print binding to the quilt.
6. Make a label and attach it to your quilt.

PILLOW TALK

Make coordinating pillowcases using directions on page 115.

Complete the look by making a throw pillow using the basic directions on pages 115–16. Make one Evening Star block as the center of the pillow top, then add 3½" borders to frame the pillow.

Streusel-Topped Pumpkin Muffins

INGREDIENTS

+ 1½ cups all-purpose flour
+ ¾ cup old-fashioned oats
+ 2 teaspoons baking powder
+ 2 teaspoons freshly grated orange peel
+ 1 teaspoon pumpkin pie spice or ground cinnamon
+ ½ teaspoon baking soda
+ ⅛ teaspoon salt
+ ½ cup currants or raisins
+ 1 egg, slightly beaten
+ ¾ cup milk
+ ¾ cup canned pumpkin
+ ½ cup firmly packed brown sugar
+ ¼ cup vegetable oil
+ Streusel Topping (see following)

RECIPE TIP: The secret to avoiding crusty edges on homemade muffins is to grease the muffin cups on the bottoms and only halfway up the sides. The muffins will be nicely rounded without those unwanted rims.

DIRECTIONS

1. Preheat the oven to 400°F (205°C). Grease 12 (2½") muffin cups; set aside.

2. For muffins, in a medium-size bowl, combine the flour, oats, baking powder, orange peel, the pumpkin pie spice, baking soda, and salt. Stir in currants. Make a well in the center of the flour mixture.

3. In another medium-size bowl, combine egg, milk, pumpkin, brown sugar, and oil. Add to flour mixture, stirring only until dry ingredients are moistened. (The batter should still be lumpy.)

4. Spoon batter into prepared muffin cups until each is about two-thirds full. Sprinkle batter with Streusel Topping. Bake 20 to 25 minutes or until golden brown and a wooden pick inserted in the center comes out clean. Let stand in muffin pan on a wire rack 5 minutes. Remove from the muffin cups. Serve warm or at room temperature with butter. Makes 12 muffins.

STREUSEL TOPPING: For streusel topping, in a small bowl, combine ⅓ cup packed brown sugar, ¼ cup all-purpose flour, and ½ teaspoon pumpkin pie spice. Using a pastry cutter or 2 knives, cut in 2 tablespoons butter until mixture resembles coarse crumbs.

Welcome Home

Quilters love to browse in antique shops. On one of her trips, my friend Barbara Burnham found delightful blocks—pieced blue houses with bright red chimneys. In another shop she found coordinating blue Nine Patch blocks. The blocks were started as different quilts, but Barbara realized they belonged together and gave them new life. When she ran out of Nine Patch blocks for the border she had planned, she made a Star block using vintage fabric scraps. The blocks are traditional, but the quilt story is unique.

House blocks always make me feel warm and cozy. What a great quilt for welcoming guests! Serve Cottage Potatoes for breakfast and make them feel at home.

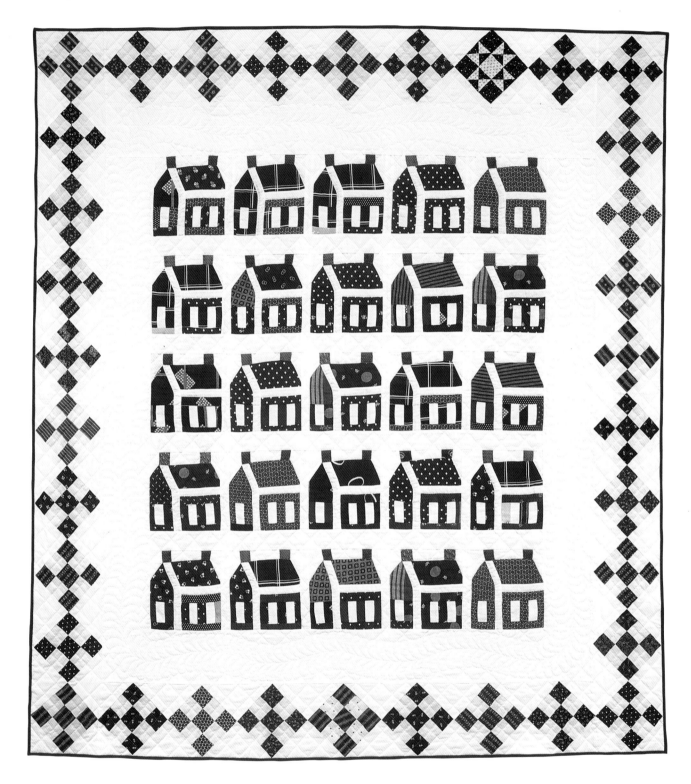

Welcome Home

By Barbara Burnham, Columbia, Maryland, 1989.

Finished Quilt Size: 57⅞" x 64¼"
Finished Block Sizes: House 7" x 7"
                       Nine Patch 4½" x 4½"
                       Star 4½" x 4½"

Materials

Yardage is based on 42"-wide fabric.

4½ yds. off-white fabric for blocks and background
2½ yds. *total* of assorted blue prints for blocks
¾ yd. red solid for blocks and binding
3¾ yds. for backing
62" x 68" piece of batting

Cutting

All measurements include ¼"-wide seam allowances. Patterns for templates A–E are on page 80.

From the off-white fabric, cut on the length-wise grain:

- 2 strips, 4½" x 45½"
- 2 strips, 3½" x 43½"
- 4 strips, 2½" x 39½"

From the remaining off-white fabric, cut on the crosswise grain:

- 25 *each* of pieces A, B, and C
- 8 strips, 1½" x 42"
- 1 strip, 3½" x 42"
- 1 strip, 4¾" x 42"; crosscut into 25 pieces, 1¼" x 4¾"
- 1 strip, 4½" x 42"; crosscut into 25 pieces, 1¼" x 4½"
- 20 strips, 1½" x 7½"
- 8 strips, 2" x 42", for the Nine Patch block
- 2 squares, 2¾" x 2¾"; cut each square twice diagonally to make 8 triangles for the Star block
- 1 square, 2" x 2", for the Star block
- 68 squares, 4⅛" x 4⅛"; cut each square once diagonally to make 136 setting triangles

From the red solid fabric, cut:

- 2 strips, 1½" x 42"
- 7 binding strips, 2" x 42"

From the assorted blue prints, cut:

- 25 *each* of pieces D and E
- 4 strips, 1" x 42", for the House block
- 25 rectangles, 1¼" x 2½"
- 25 rectangles, 2" x 2½"
- 6 strips, 1¼" x 42"
- 50 rectangles, 1¼" x 4¾", for the House blocks
- 10 strips, 2" x 42", for the Nine Patch blocks
- 2 squares, 2¾" x 2¾"; cut each square twice diagonally to make 8 triangles for the Star block
- 4 squares, 2" x 2", for the Star Block

Making the Pieced House Blocks

You need 25 House blocks for this quilt.

1. Sew 1½"- and 3½"-wide off-white strips and 1½"-wide red strips together as shown. Press the seams toward the red strips. Use a ruler and rotary cutter to clean-cut the edges of the strip set. Crosscut the strips into 1½"-wide segments; cut 25 segments. This is the chimney area.

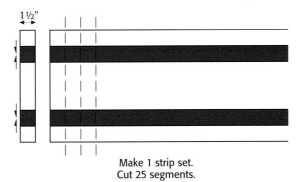

Make 1 strip set.
Cut 25 segments.

2. Join pieces A–E as shown to make the roof area.

3. Sew a 1"-wide blue strip to either side of a 1½"-wide off-white strip. Make 2 of these strip sets. Crosscut the strip sets into 2¼"-wide segments; cut 25 segments.

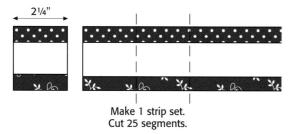

2¼"

Make 1 strip set.
Cut 25 segments.

4. Sew a 2" x 2½" blue rectangle and a 1¼" x 2½" blue rectangle to the top and bottom of each unit to make the door area. Repeat to make 25 of these units.

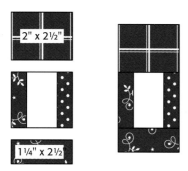

2" x 2½"

1¼" x 2½"

5. Sew 2 off-white 1½" x 42" strips and 3 blue 1¼" x 42" strips together as shown. Make 2 of these strip sets. Crosscut the strips into 2¼"-wide segments; cut 25 segments.

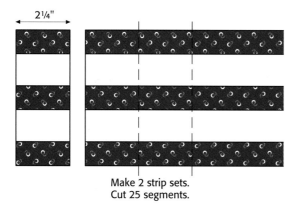

2¼"

Make 2 strip sets.
Cut 25 segments.

6. Sew a 1¼" x 4¾" blue rectangle to the top and bottom of the segments cut in step 5 to make the window units.

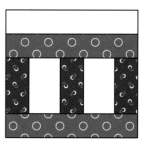

7. Sew a 1¼" x 4¾" off-white rectangle to the top of each window unit.

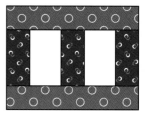

8. Sew the door unit from step 4 and the window unit from step 7 to either side of a 1¼" x 4½" off-white strip. Repeat for all 25 houses.

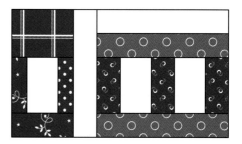

9. Add the roof and chimney sections to the window and door sections to complete 25 House blocks.

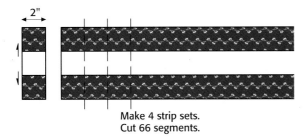

House Block
Make 25.

Making the Nine Patch Blocks

You need 33 Nine Patch blocks for the quilt border.

1. Sew a 2"-wide blue strip to each long edge of a 2"-wide off-white strip. Press the seams toward the blue strips. Make 4 strip sets. Use a ruler and rotary cutter to clean-cut the edges of the strip set. Crosscut the strips into 2"-wide segments; cut 66 segments.

2"

Make 4 strip sets.
Cut 66 segments.

2. Sew a 2"-wide off-white strip to each long edge of a 2"-wide blue strip. Press the seams toward the blue strips. Make 2 of these strip sets. Use a ruler and rotary cutter to clean-cut the edges of the strip set. Crosscut the strips into 2"-wide segments; cut 33 segments.

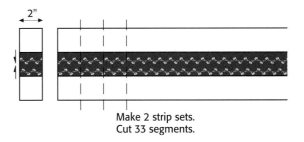

2"

Make 2 strip sets.
Cut 33 segments.

3. Join 2 segments from step 1 and 1 segment from step 2 to complete a block. Make a total of 33 Nine Patch blocks.

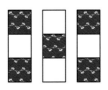

Nine Patch Block
Make 33.

4. Sew off-white setting triangles to opposite sides of the Nine Patch blocks as shown. Sew 2 more setting triangles to the remaining sides to make 33 border squares.

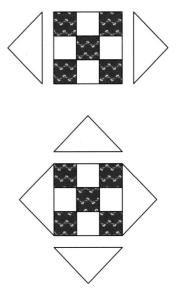

Making the Star Block

You need one Star block for the quilt border.

1. Sew 2¾" off-white and blue triangles together as shown to make 4 small pieced squares.

2. Sew the pieced squares and 2" blue and off-white squares together as shown to make a Star block.

**Star Block
Make 1.**

3. Sew off-white setting triangles to opposite sides of the Star block as shown. Sew 2 more setting triangles to the remaining sides to complete the Star border square.

Assembling the Quilt

1. Arrange the House blocks and 1½" x 7½" off-white sashing strips as shown. Using 5 pieced blocks and 4 sashing strips per row, sew 5 rows as shown.

2. Place 2½" x 39½" off-white setting strips between the rows of House blocks and sew the rows together.

Adding the Borders

1. Sew the 3½" x 43½" off-white side borders to opposite sides of the quilt.
2. Sew the 4½" x 45½" off-white borders to the top and bottom of the quilt.
3. Sew 7 Nine Patch blocks together as shown for the bottom border. Sew this border to the quilt.

Bottom Border

4. Sew 6 Nine Patch blocks and the Star block together for the top border, as shown. Attach this border to the top of the quilt.

Top Border

5. Sew 2 rows each with 10 Nine Patch blocks. Sew these side borders to the quilt.

Finishing

1. Mark the quilt top with a design of your choice.
2. Piece the backing horizontally to fit the quilt top.
3. Layer the quilt top with batting and backing; baste the layers together.
4. Hand or machine quilt as desired.
5. Trim the batting and backing even with the edges of the quilt top. Sew the red binding strips to the quilt.
6. Make a label and attach it to your quilt.

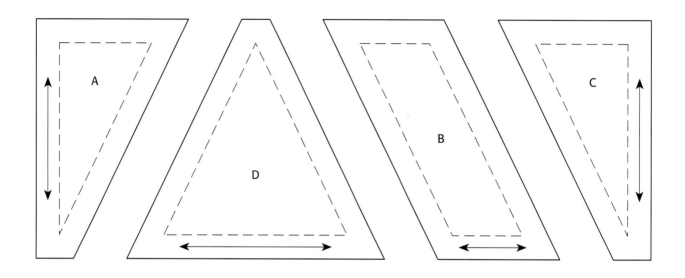

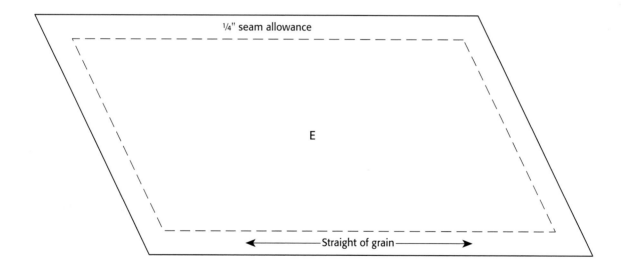

¼" seam allowance

Straight of grain

Cottage Potatoes

INGREDIENTS

- ¼ cup butter
- 1 cup chopped onion
- ½ cup chopped red bell pepper (optional)
- 1 tablespoon snipped fresh sage or 1 teaspoon dried sage, crushed
- ½ teaspoon salt
- ¼ teaspoon black pepper
- 1 (8-ounce) carton low-fat dairy sour cream
- 1 tablespoon all-purpose flour
- 2 (18-ounce) packages refrigerated diced potatoes
- 1½ cups herb-seasoned croutons, coarsely crushed
- 2 cups (8 ounces) shredded cheddar cheese
- 1 cup milk
- ¼ cup snipped fresh parsley

DIRECTIONS

1. Preheat the oven to 350°F (175°C). Lightly grease a 13" x 9" x 2" baking dish; set aside.
2. In a large skillet, melt butter over medium heat. Add onion, bell pepper, sage, salt, and black pepper and cook, stirring frequently, 5 to 8 minutes or until vegetables are tender.
3. In a large bowl, combine sour cream and flour. Stir in onion mixture, potatoes, croutons, half of the cheese, the milk, and half of the parsley. Place potato mixture in the prepared dish.
4. Cover and bake 40 minutes. Sprinkle remaining cheese and parsley over top. Bake, uncovered, 10 to 15 minutes or until heated through. Remove from oven. Makes 8 servings.

RECIPE TIP: If you wish to substitute whole potatoes for the refrigerated diced potatoes, use 6 to 7 medium-size potatoes (about 2 pounds). Place potatoes in a large saucepan. Add enough water to cover potatoes and, if desired, ¼ teaspoon salt; bring to a boil. Reduce heat, cover, and simmer 20 to 25 minutes or until tender. Drain well; cool slightly. Peel and cut potatoes into ½" cubes. Continue as directed above.

Vintage Memories

Take your guests on a trip into the past with a collection of new fabrics that look vintage. The scrappy reproduction prints include colors from the heritage of American quilts—indigo blue, Turkey red, cheddar gold, and double pink. A touch of appliqué across the pillow area and border adds vines, leaves, flowers, birds, berries, and pineapples, a symbol of colonial hospitality. Whether this quilt tops an antique bed with carved pineapples or something a little more modern, it will welcome your guests with a feeling of tradition and comfort.

Vintage Memories

Designed by Mimi Dietrich. Pieced and appliquéd by the Vintage Quilters: Shelly Cornwell, Karan Flanscha, Nancy Hayes, Barbara Jacobson, Sharri Nottger, Robin Venter; Waterloo and Cedar Falls, Iowa; 2002. Machine quilted by Joyce Kuehl.

Finished Quilt Size: 91⅝" x 100½"
Finished Block Size: 4" x 4"
Diagonal Block Measurement: 5⅝"

Materials

Yardage is based on 42"-wide fabric.

5 yds. *total* of assorted reproduction prints, including golds, blues, reds, pinks, yellows, purples, blacks, and greens, for blocks and appliqué
6½ yds. tan print for setting blocks, triangles, and borders
½ yd. plum print for inner borders
1½ yds. dark green print for appliquéd vines and binding
8⅝ yds. fabric for backing
96" x 105 " piece of batting

Cutting

All measurements include ¼"-wide seam allowances. Patterns for the flowers, leaves, berries, birds, and pineapple are on pages 89–91.

From the assorted reproduction prints, cut:

• 190 squares, 5" x 5"; cut each square into 4 squares, 2½" x 2½" (760 total squares; 380 pairs)

Cut the remaining assorted reproduction prints as follows:

From a gold print, cut:

• 3 pineapples

From a blue print, cut:

• 6 birds
• 6 bird wings

From a pink print, cut:

• 12 flowers

From a yellow print, cut:

• 12 flower centers

From a purple print, cut:

• 54 berries

From the assorted green prints, cut:

• 73 leaves

From the tan print, cut on the lengthwise grain:

• 2 strips, 8½" x 104"
• 1 strip, 8½" x 95"

From the remaining tan print, cut:

• 23 strips, 4½" x 42"; crosscut strips into 180 squares, 4½" x 4½"
• 14 squares, 6⅞" x 6⅞"; cut each square twice diagonally to make 56 side setting triangles (There will be 2 extra.)
• 2 squares, 3¾" x 3¾"; cut each square once diagonally to make 4 corner setting triangles

From the plum print, cut:

• 10 strips, 1½" x 42"

From the dark green print, cut:

• 10 binding strips, 2" x 42"
• ⅝"-wide bias strips (8 yds. total length)

Making the Four Patch Blocks

You need 190 Four Patch blocks for this quilt.

1. Separate the 2½" squares into 380 matching pairs. Arrange 2 pairs to make each block.

2. Sew 2 squares together; then join the pairs to make a Four Patch block. Repeat to make 190 Four Patch blocks.

Four Patch Block
Make 190.

Assembling the Quilt

1. Arrange the Four Patch blocks and 4½" tan squares and setting triangles in rows as shown. Lay the blocks out on a floor or design wall to help you distribute the colors evenly. You should have 13 vertical rows of Four Patch blocks set on point, with 16 blocks in each row (except for in the "pillow" top area).

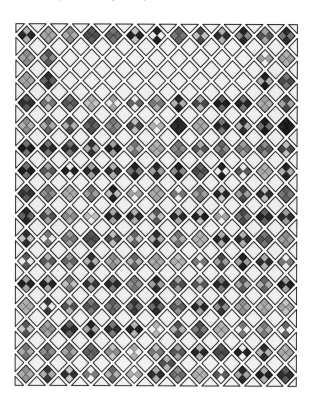

2. Referring to the illustration below, sew the blocks together into 3 large units. This assembly will make it easier for you to appliqué the pillow design before sewing the entire quilt together.

3. Photocopy the appliqué border patterns A, B, and C on pages 89–91 and tape them together using the pillow panel vine line. Trace the pineapple in the center of the pillow panel; then trace the vines on either side. Use a light box to trace the design in reverse on the left side of the pineapple.

4. Fold the long edges of the ⅝" dark green bias strips into the center of the strips, wrong sides together so that the raw edges meet. Baste along the edges with small stitches to make the vines. Gently pull on one of the basting threads to ease the bias strip into a curved shape.

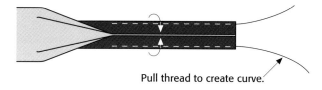

Pull thread to create curve.

5. Appliqué the vines, leaves, flowers, berries, and birds using your favorite appliqué techniques.

Pillow Tuck Appliqué

6. When the appliqué is complete, sew the 3 units together to make the center of the quilt.

Adding the Borders

1. Sew the plum print border strips together end to end to make the inner borders. From the long strip, cut 1 strip 75⅝" long and sew it to the top of the quilt.

    Cut 1 strip 95" long and sew it to the inner edge of the 95"-long tan border strip. Cut 2 strips 104" long and sew them to the inner edges of the 104"-long tan border strips.

2. Matching the plum edges of the borders to the top of the quilt, sew the 104"-long side borders to the edges of the quilt, stopping ¼" from the bottom corner. Make sure the plum borders are attached to the quilt top, not the tan ones.

3. Sew the 95"-long border to the bottom of the quilt, again making sure the plum border is attached to the quilt top. Stop sewing ¼" from the corners.

4. Miter the 2 bottom quilt corners, referring to the directions on page 122.

5. Photocopy the appliqué border patterns A, B, and C (on pages 89–91) and tape them together using the border vine line.

6. Trace the pineapple in the center of the mitered corner; then trace the vines on either side. Use a light box to trace the design in reverse on the left side of the pineapple.

7. Appliqué the vines, leaves, flowers, berries, and birds using your favorite appliqué techniques.

Border Appliqué

Finishing

1. Mark the quilt top with a design of your choice.
2. Piece the backing horizontally to fit the quilt top.
3. Layer the quilt top with batting and backing; baste the layers together.
4. Hand or machine quilt as desired.
5. Trim the batting and backing even with the edges of the quilt top. Sew the dark green print binding strips to the quilt.
6. Make a label and attach it to your quilt.

Chocolate–Pecan Cinnamon Rolls

INGREDIENTS

- 6¾ to 7¼ cups all-purpose flour
- 1½ cups warm milk (105° to 115°F; 40° to 45°C)
- 1 tablespoon sugar
- 2 (¼-ounce) packages active dry yeast
- 3 eggs
- ½ cup sugar
- ⅓ cup unsweetened cocoa powder
- 1 tablespoon freshly grated orange peel
- 1 teaspoon salt
- ½ cup butter, at room temperature, cut into pieces
- Sugar-Cinnamon Filling (see below)
- ½ cup miniature semisweet chocolate pieces
- ½ cup chopped pecans
- Chocolate Icing (see below)

DIRECTIONS

1. In a large bowl, combine 3 cups of flour, the milk, 1 tablespoon of sugar, and the yeast. Beat with an electric mixer at medium speed 2 minutes or until smooth. (The mixture will be thick and sticky.) Cover with plastic wrap. Let stand at room temperature 30 minutes or until bubbly.

2. Add eggs, ½ cup sugar, cocoa powder, orange peel, and salt to flour mixture; stir in another cup of flour. Beat with an electric mixer at medium speed 2 minutes or until smooth. Add butter, and beat until well combined. Using a wooden spoon, stir in as much of the remaining flour as needed to make a soft dough.

3. Turn out onto a lightly floured surface. Knead 5 to 6 minutes or until dough is smooth and elastic, adding only enough of the remaining flour to prevent sticking. Clean and butter the bowl. Place dough in bowl, turning dough to coat all surfaces. Cover with a slightly damp towel. Let rise in a warm place, free from drafts, 1 hour or until doubled in bulk.

4. While dough is rising, prepare Sugar-Cinnamon Filling; set aside. Lightly grease a 13" x 9" x 2" baking pan; set aside.

5. Punch down dough. Turn out onto lightly floured surface. Cover dough; let stand 10 minutes. Roll out dough into a 16" x 12" rectangle. Spread filling over dough. Sprinkle with miniature chocolate pieces and pecans. Beginning on a long side, roll tightly in jellyroll fashion. Pinch the seam to seal. Cut the roll into 12 slices. Arrange, cut side down, in the prepared pan. Cover with a dry towel. Let rise in a warm place, free from drafts, 30 minutes or until nearly double in bulk.

6. Preheat the oven to 375°F (190°C). Bake 20 to 25 minutes or until browned. While rolls are baking, prepare Chocolate Icing. Invert rolls onto a wire rack. Cool slightly. Spread rolls with icing. Makes 12 rolls.

SUGAR-CINNAMON FILLING: In a small bowl, stir together ½ cup sugar, ¼ cup (½ stick) melted butter, 1 tablespoon ground cinnamon, and 2 teaspoons all-purpose flour.

CHOCOLATE ICING: In a small saucepan, melt ¾ cup milk chocolate pieces and 3 tablespoons butter over low heat, stirring frequently. Remove from heat. Stir in 1½ cups sifted powdered sugar and 3 tablespoons hot water. If needed, stir in additional hot water to make a smooth and creamy icing of spreading consistency.

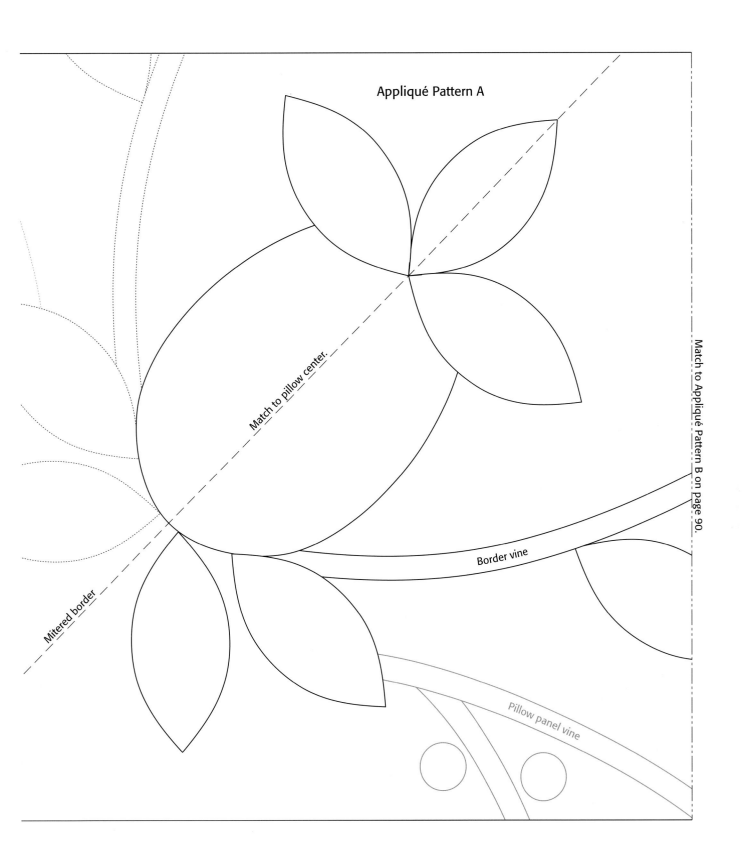

Appliqué Pattern A

Match to pillow center.

Mitered border

Border vine

Pillow panel vine

Match to Appliqué Pattern B on page 90.

Match to Appliqué Pattern C on page 91.

Appliqué Pattern B

Match to Appliqué Pattern A on page 89.

Appliqué Pattern C

Match to Appliqué Pattern B on page 90.

Wish upon a Star

Patchwork is so much fun! Squares and triangles pieced together become beautiful designs, and perhaps the most popular of all is the star.

In this star design, beautiful large-scale floral prints are used in large blocks to create a quilt that is fast and easy to make and that looks great on a bed. The floral fabrics and coordinating color prints set the tone for welcoming guests into a cozy cottage room. If you live in a cold-climate region, consider making this quilt with flannels for extra warmth.

Whatever fabrics you choose, position the star in the center of the bed and make a wish before you crawl under the covers!

Wish upon a Star

By Monday Night Madness: Joan Costello, Mimi Dietrich, Laurie Gregg, Phyllis Hess, Barbara McMahon,
Vivian Schafer; Baltimore, Maryland; 2002. Machine quilted by Laurie Gregg, Ellicott City, Maryland.

Finished Quilt Size: 89½" x 107½"
Finished Block Size: 9" x 9"

Materials

Yardage is based on 42"-wide fabric.
5½ yds. tan floral for blocks and border
3½ yds. dark red floral for blocks and border
3½ yds. blue print for blocks, border, and binding
8¼ yds. fabric for backing
94" x 112" piece of batting

Cutting

All measurements include ¼"-wide seam allowances.

From the dark red floral, cut on the lengthwise grain:
- 2 strips, 7½" x 93½"
- 2 strips, 7½" x 89½"

From the remaining dark red floral, cut:
- 3 strips, 9½" x 42"; cut into 12 squares, 9½" x 9½"

From the tan floral, cut on the lengthwise grain:
  2 strips, 4½" x 85½"
  2 strips, 4½" x 75½"

From the remaining tan floral, cut:
- 5 strips, 9½" x 42"; cut into 20 squares, 9½" x 9½"
- 6 strips, 10½" x 42"; cut into 16 squares, 10½" x 10½". Cut each square twice diagonally to make 64 triangles.

From the blue print, cut from the lengthwise grain:
- 2 strips, 2½" x 81½"
- 2 strips, 2½" x 67½"

From the remaining blue print, cut:
- 6 strips, 10½" x 42"; cut into 16 squares, 10½" x 10½". Cut each square twice diagonally to make 64 triangles.
- 11 binding strips, 2" x 42"

Making the Hourglass Blocks

You need 31 Hourglass blocks for this quilt.

1. Sew a tan triangle to a blue triangle along the short edges as shown.

2. Sew 2 pieced triangles together to make an Hourglass block. Repeat to make a total of 31 blocks.

Hourglass Block
Make 31.

Assembling the Quilt

1. Make 5 rows alternating four 9½" tan squares and 3 Hourglass blocks as shown.

Make 5 rows.

2. Make 4 rows alternating 4 Hourglass blocks and three 9½" dark red squares as shown.

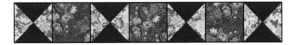

Make 4 rows.

3. Referring to the quilt photograph on page 94, sew the rows together, beginning and ending with a tan row.

Adding the Borders

1. Sew the 2½" x 81½" blue border strips to opposite sides of the quilt. Sew the 2½" x 67½" blue border strips to the top and bottom of the quilt. Press all seams toward the borders.

2. Sew the 4½" x 85½" tan border strips to opposite sides of the quilt. Sew the 4½" x 75½" tan border strips to the top and bottom of the quilt. Press the seams toward the tan borders.

3. Sew the 7½" x 93½" dark red border strips to opposite sides of the quilt. Sew the 7½" x 89½" dark red border strips to the top and bottom of the quilt. Press the seams toward the dark red borders.

Finishing

1. Mark the quilt top with a design of your choice.
2. Piece the backing horizontally to fit the quilt top.
3. Layer the quilt top with batting and backing; baste the layers together.
4. Hand or machine quilt as desired.
5. Trim the batting and backing even with the edges of the quilt top. Sew the blue print binding strips to the quilt.
6. Make a label and attach it to your quilt.

Brunch Fruit Parfaits

INGREDIENTS

+ ¼ cup orange juice
+ ¼ cup sugar
+ ⅛ teaspoon ground cinnamon
+ ⅛ teaspoon ground nutmeg
+ ¾ cup cranberries
+ ¾ cup unsweetened applesauce
+ 3 ripe kiwifruit, peeled and sliced
+ 1 large ripe mango, peeled and sliced, or 2 medium-firm bananas, peeled and sliced
+ 2 medium-size oranges, peeled and sectioned
+ 1 (8-ounce) carton peach-flavored yogurt or other flavored yogurt
+ Carambola (star fruit) slices (garnish)

DIRECTIONS

1. In a small saucepan, combine orange juice, sugar, cinnamon, and nutmeg. Cook and stir over medium heat, stirring with a wooden spoon to dissolve sugar. Add cranberries and bring to a boil. Reduce heat and cook, stirring often, 3 to 4 minutes or until cranberries pop. Remove from heat; cool slightly. Stir in applesauce. Cover and chill in the refrigerator 30 minutes.

2. In 6 clear parfait glasses, arrange kiwi slices, pressing flat to stick to the sides of the glasses. Spoon in chilled cranberry mixture. Top with mango slices and orange sections. Top with yogurt. Cover and chill 1 hour.

3. To serve, garnish rim of each glass with a slice of carambola. Makes 6 servings.

Twilight in the Garden

After a day of sewing or gardening with friends, cuddle up under this scrap quilt made from coordinating fabrics. The muted colors provide a soothing palette of patchwork to relax the mind and body. And with such a variety of colors, this quilt can coordinate with any room.

"Twilight in the Garden" is just the right opportunity to combine a favorite collection of fabric with patchwork and appliqué techniques. Many quilters collect fat quarters—quarter-yard pieces of fabric cut 18" x 20". Fat quarters are available in quilt shops, at quilt shows, and often at guild meetings. Quilters trade them, give them as presents, and occasionally they even use them to make quilts!

If you love the combination of patchwork and appliqué, why not get started on this quilt right now? Your guests will rest well under this comfy quilt when twilight signals the end of a perfect day.

Twilight in the Garden

Designed and appliquéd by Mimi Dietrich. Pieced by Mimi Dietrich and Emily Watson, Baltimore, Maryland, 2002.
Machine quilted by Linda Newsom, Crofton, Maryland.

Finished Quilt Size: 89½" x 99½"
Finished Block Size: 5" x 5"

Materials

Yardage is based on 42"-wide fabric unless otherwise noted.

22 fat quarters of assorted green, blue, brown, and gold prints for blocks and appliquéd leaves

6 fat quarters of assorted red prints for blocks and appliquéd hearts

½ yd. each of 8 assorted light prints for blocks

3 yds. light print for outer border

3 yds. dark green print for inner border, appliquéd border vine, and binding

8½ yds. fabric for backing

94" x 104" piece of batting

Cutting

All measurements include ¼"-wide seam allowances. Patterns for the leaves and hearts are on pages 104–105.

From each of the 8 assorted light prints, cut:
- 42 squares, 3⅜" x 3⅜"; cut each square once diagonally to make 84 small triangles (672 total)

From *each* of the 22 assorted print fat quarters, cut:
- 4 squares, 5⅞" x 5⅞"; cut each square once diagonally to make 8 large triangles (176 total)
- 4 squares, 3⅜" x 3⅜"; cut each square once diagonally to make 8 small triangles (176 total)
- 6 leaves (132 total)

From *each* of the 6 assorted red print fat quarters, cut:
- 4 squares, 5⅞" x 5⅞"; cut each square once diagonally to make 8 large triangles (48 total)
- 4 squares, 3⅜" x 3⅜"; cut each square once diagonally to make 8 small triangles (48 total)
- 6 hearts for border vine appliqué (36 total)

From the light border print, cut on the lengthwise grain:
- 2 strips, 8½" x 104"
- 2 strips, 8½" x 94"

From the dark green print, cut on the lengthwise grain:
- 2 strips, 2" x 80½"
- 2 strips, 2" x 73½"

From the remaining dark green print, cut:
- 11 binding strips, 2" x 42"
- ⅝"-wide bias strips (12 yds. total length)

Making the Patchwork Blocks

You need 224 blocks for this quilt. Each block uses one light print and one dark print cut from any of the fat quarters.

1. Sew a small light triangle to a small dark triangle. Press the seams toward the dark triangle.

2. Sew matching small light triangles to each dark side of the pieced square as shown. Press the seams toward the light triangles.

3. Sew a matching large dark triangle to the pieced triangle. Press the seams toward the dark triangle to complete a Flying Goose block.

Flying Goose Block
Make 224.

4. Repeat steps 1–3 to make 224 blocks.

Appliquéing the Borders

Appliqué the borders before sewing them to the quilt. Appliqué the corners after you attach the borders to the quilt.

1. Make 15 photocopies of the border appliqué pattern on page 104. Tape 8 patterns together for the side borders. Tape 7 patterns together for the top and bottom borders.

Tape together 8 repeats for side borders
and 7 repeats for top and bottom borders.

2. Center the 8½" x 104" light border strips over the side border appliqué pattern (with 8 repeats) and trace the design onto the fabric. Repeat for the 8½" x 94" top and bottom border strips, using the pattern with 7 repeats.

3. Prepare the vines and appliqué them in place. Fold the long edges of the ⅝" dark green bias strips into the center of the strips, wrong sides together, so that the raw edges meet. Baste along the edges with small stitches to make the vines. Gently pull on one of the basting threads to ease the bias strip into a curved shape. At the end of each vine, turn the fabric under ¼" and appliqué. Position the next vine, turn under ¼", and appliqué the ends together.

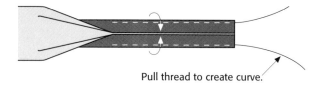

Pull thread to create curve.

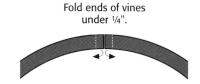

Fold ends of vines
under ¼".

4. Appliqué the leaves and hearts along the vine using your favorite appliqué technique.

Assembling the Quilt

1. Referring to the photograph on page 100, arrange the blocks so that all the dark triangles point in the same direction. You should have 16 rows, each with 14 blocks across.

2. Sew the blocks together in rows; then sew the rows together.

Adding the Borders

1. Sew the 2" x 80½" dark green inner border strips to opposite sides of the quilt. Sew the 2" x 73½" dark green inner border strips to the top and bottom of the quilt. Press all seams toward the dark green borders.

2. Center the appliquéd borders on the edges of the quilt. Sew the borders to the edges of the quilt, stopping ¼" from the corner. (The borders are a few inches longer than the edges to allow for mitering.) Miter the 4 quilt corners, referring to the directions on page 122.

3. Position the corner appliqué pattern (page 105) under the corner of the quilt. Trace the corner design onto the quilt. Appliqué the remaining vines and hearts. Repeat for the remaining 3 corners.

Finishing

1. Mark the quilt top with a design of your choice.
2. Piece the backing horizontally to fit the quilt top.
3. Layer the quilt top with batting and backing; baste the layers together.
4. Hand or machine quilt as desired.
5. Trim the batting and backing even with the edges of the quilt top. Sew the dark green print binding to the quilt.
6. Make a label and attach it to your quilt.

Spinach and Ham Quiche

INGREDIENTS

- 1 (9") folded refrigerated unbaked piecrust
- 1 tablespoon butter
- 1 cup sliced fresh mushrooms
- 4 green onions, sliced
- ½ of a (10-ounce) package frozen chopped spinach, thawed and well drained
- ½ cup chopped fully cooked ham
- 3 eggs, lightly beaten
- 1 cup half-and-half or light cream
- ¼ teaspoon salt
- ⅛ teaspoon ground nutmeg
- 1½ cups (6 ounces) shredded Swiss or cheddar cheese
- 1 tablespoon all-purpose flour

DIRECTIONS

1. Preheat the oven to 450°F (230°C). Let piecrust stand at room temperature according to package directions.

2. Unfold piecrust and ease into a 9" pie plate. Fold edge under and flute as desired. Line pastry with double thickness of foil. Bake 5 minutes. Carefully remove foil. Bake 4 to 5 minutes more or until pastry is firm on the bottom and side. Remove from oven; set aside. Reduce oven temperature to 325°F (165°C).

3. In a large skillet, melt butter over medium heat. Add mushrooms and onions and cook, stirring frequently, 5 minutes or until mushrooms are tender; drain well. Stir in well-drained spinach and ham; set aside.

4. In a large bowl, stir together eggs, half-and-half, salt, and nutmeg. Stir mushroom mixture into egg mixture.

5. Toss together shredded cheese and flour; stir into egg-and-vegetable mixture. Carefully pour mixture into pastry shell. Bake 40 to 50 minutes or until a knife inserted near the center comes out clean. If necessary, cover edge of crust with foil to prevent overbrowning. Let stand 10 minutes before cutting into wedges. Makes 6 servings.

RECIPE NOTE: For well-drained spinach, place thawed spinach in a colander or sieve. With the back of a spoon, press out the excess liquid. Pat spinach dry with paper towels.

Border Appliqué Pattern

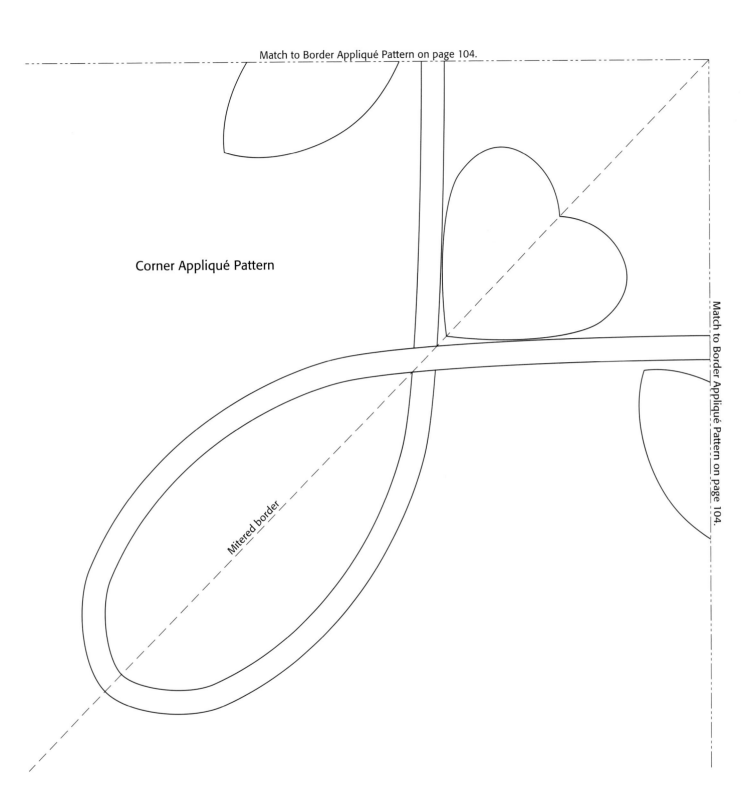

Match to Border Appliqué Pattern on page 104.

Corner Appliqué Pattern

Mitered border

Match to Border Appliqué Pattern on page 104.

And to All a Good Night

All quilters fall in love with fabulous fabrics and use them to make quilts. Sometimes, however, we find fabrics that we just can't cut into small pieces because we love the beautiful colors, textures, or patterns. "And to All a Good Night" is an ideal project to showcase just such a special fabric.

This holiday quilt was inspired by the traditional Amish Center Diamond design that is noted for its large square of solid fabric set on point in the middle of the quilt top. Substituting a large-scale floral fabric for the solid is very striking. If you like, you can use a heavier decorator fabric for this quilt because there are only a few seams. And of course, you can use fabric appropriate for any time of the year. The design is fast and easy to sew and the dramatic results look great on a bed. Make pillowcases to match, and your guests will be ready for a perfect good night!

And to All a Good Night

By Mimi Dietrich, Baltimore, Maryland, 2002. Machine quilted by Linda Newsom, Crofton, Maryland.

Finished Quilt Size: 96½" x 96½"
Center Block Size: 34½" x 34½"

Materials

Yardage is based on 42"-wide fabric.

5¼ yds. floral print for center square, setting
   triangles, and borders
3 yds. green print for sashing strips, border, and
   binding
1 yd. red print for setting squares
9 yds. fabric for backing
2½ yds. off-white fabric for pillowcases
101" x 101" piece of batting
Red embroidery floss

Cutting

All measurements include ¼"-wide seam allowances.

From the green print, cut:
• 4 strips, 4½" x 35"
• 4 strips, 8½" x 60½", cut on the lengthwise grain
• 10 binding strips, 2" x 42"

From the floral print, cut:
• 1 square, 35" x 35" (To cut a perfect 35" square,
   fold a 36" square neatly in quarters and cut a 17½"
   square, measuring carefully from the folded edges.)
• 2 squares, 31" x 31"; cut each square once diagonally to make 4 setting triangles
• 4 strips, 10½" x 76½", cut on the lengthwise
   grain★

*★These cutting dimensions assume you have 42" of usable
width; check your fabric first. Some fabrics are narrower
and you may want to cut your borders slightly narrower to
compensate.*

From the red print, cut:
• 4 squares, 4½" x 4½"
• 4 squares, 8½" x 8½"
• 4 squares, 10½" x 10½"

Assembling the Quilt Center

1. Sew a 4½" x 35" green sashing strip to opposite
   sides of the 35" floral square.

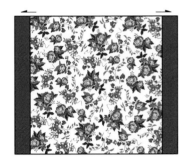

2. Sew a 4½" red square to opposite ends of the 2
   remaining 4½" x 35" green sashing strips.

3. Sew the sashing strips to the 2 remaining sides of
   the floral center square.

4. Sew a floral triangle to opposite sides of the quilt center. Press the seams toward the triangles. Add floral triangles to the remaining sides to complete the center. Press.

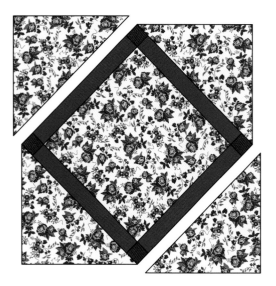

Adding the Borders

1. Sew the 8½" x 60½" green border strips to opposite sides of the quilt.
2. Sew an 8½" red square to each end of the 2 remaining green border strips; then sew these border strips to the top and bottom of the quilt to complete the inner border.
3. Sew the 10½" x 76½" floral border strips to opposite sides of the quilt.
4. Sew a 10½" red square to each end of the 2 remaining floral border strips; then sew these border strips to the top and bottom of the quilt.

Finishing

1. Mark the quilt top with a design of your choice.
2. Piece the backing vertically to fit the quilt top.
3. Layer the quilt top with batting and backing; baste the layers together.
4. Hand or machine quilt as desired.
5. Trim the batting and backing even with the edges of the quilt top. Sew the green print binding to the quilt.
6. Make a label and attach it to your quilt.

PILLOW TALK

Make the holiday pillowcases using the basic directions on page 115. Trace the words and holly design on pages 112–13 onto the edge of the pillowcases. Embroider the words using a chain stitch. Appliqué the holly and berries. Or, use the appliqué and embroidery patterns to embellish purchased lace-edged pillowcases.

For a coordinating throw pillow, appliqué the holly leaves and berries on page 114 onto your background fabric, and then trace "Merry Christmas" using a fine-point permanent pen. Add 3½" red and green borders to complete the pillow top. Use the basic directions on pages 115–16 to complete your throw pillow.

Cinnamon Pillows

INGREDIENTS

+ ¾ cup sugar
+ 2 teaspoons ground cinnamon
+ 16 slices white sandwich bread
+ 1 (8-ounce) tub cream cheese (pineapple, strawberry, honey nut, or plain)
+ 1 egg yolk, lightly beaten
+ 2 teaspoons sugar
+ ¾ cup (1½ sticks) butter, melted

DIRECTIONS

1. Preheat the oven to 375°F (190°C). In a shallow dish or medium-size bowl, stir together the ¾ cup sugar and cinnamon; set aside.
2. Trim crusts from bread slices. In a small bowl, combine cream cheese, egg yolk, and the 2 teaspoons sugar. Evenly spread each slice with about 1 tablespoon of the cream cheese mixture. Roll up bread slices. With seam side down, gently slice each roll in half crosswise.
3. Dip each roll into melted butter, then roll in sugar-cinnamon mixture. Place rolls upright on a large ungreased cookie or baking sheet. Bake 10 to 12 minutes or until lightly browned. Serve warm or cool. Makes 32.

Goodnight

...stmas to All

Accessories

Many of the quilt projects in this book have accompanying pillowcases, patchwork throw pillows, or pillow shams to complete the look of the room and really make it feel as special as if you were staying at a charming bed and breakfast. You'll find the basic cutting and assembly directions for each of these items here.

Queen-Size Pillow Shams
Makes two shams.

Materials
Yardage is based on 42"- or 54"-wide fabric.

3 yds. main fabric
1 yd. contrasting fabric

Cutting
All measurements include ½"-wide seam allowances.

From the main fabric, cut:
- 2 rectangles, 21" x 31", for front
- 4 rectangles, 20" x 27", for back

From the contrasting fabric, cut:
- 4 strips, 4" x 31"
- 4 strips, 4" x 27"

Making the Pillow Sham
Use a ½" seam allowance throughout.

1. Sew the 4" x 31" borders to the 31"-long top and bottom edge of the main fabric rectangle.
2. Sew the 4" x 27" borders to the sides of the rectangle.
3. On each sham back, turn under ½" twice along one 27"-long edge and sew a hem.
4. Overlap the hemmed back pieces so they form a rectangle the same size as the sham front; baste the back pieces together.
5. Place the sham and backing right sides together, pin, and sew a ½" seam around the edges.
6. Turn the sham right side out through the back.
7. Topstitch the front along the edge of the main fabric.
8. Insert pillow.

Pillowcases

Finished Size: Standard 20" x 31"
Queen: 20" x 35"

Materials
Yardage is based on 42"- or 54"-wide fabric.

2½ yds. fabric for each pair of pillowcases

Cutting
All measurements include ¼"-wide seam allowances.

With the fabric folded in half, cut with the long edge on the fold:
- 2 rectangles, 20½" x 36", for standard size
- 2 rectangles, 20½" x 40", for queen size

Making the Pillowcases
1. Fold pillowcase fabric right sides together.
2. Starting at the fold, sew a ¼" seam along one short side; continue along one long side.
3. At the open end of the pillowcase, fold edge of fabric up ¼", wrong sides together. Press.
4. Fold up a 4" hem in the pillowcase. Press and pin. Sew along the edge of the hem to finish the pillowcase.

Patchwork Throw Pillow

Materials
Extra quilt block to match your quilt
3½"-wide strips of coordinating fabric for borders
Backing fabric 4" wider than your block plus borders (for 10" blocks, a fat quarter or ½ yard will do; for larger blocks, you'll need ¾ yard)
Pillow form the size of your quilt block

Making the Patchwork Pillow
1. Make an extra block to match your quilt design.
2. Add 3½"-wide borders around the block.

3. Cut a backing for your pillow, 4" wider than the front of the pillow.

4. Cut the backing in half. Turn under ¼" twice along the 2 center edges you just cut and sew a narrow hem.

5. Overlap the hemmed back pieces so they are the same size as the front and baste them together.

6. Place the pillow and backing right sides together, pin, and sew a ¼" seam around the edges.

7. Turn the pillow right side out through the back opening.

8. Topstitch along the edge of the quilt block.

9. Stuff with a pillow form. (You can make your own pillow form using 2 squares of muslin the same size as your quilt block. Sew around the edges; leave an opening, and stuff with polyfill.)

Dust Ruffle

Materials

1 flat sheet, trimmed to the size of your mattress plus 1"

Fabric for ruffle as follows:

To determine the amount of decorator fabric you need, measure the length and width of your bed. Take 2 times the length, plus the width, for total yardage. Example: queen size mattress is 80" long x 2 = 160" + 60" wide = 220" ÷ 36" = 6.11 or 6¼ yards.

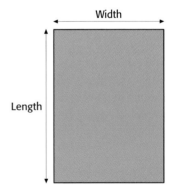

(Length x 2) + width = Total yardage

Making the Dust Ruffle

1. Cut the dust-ruffle fabric in half lengthwise and remove the selvages.

2. Sew 2 short ends of the fabric together using a ½" seam allowance to make 1 long strip.

3. Sew a 1" hem in the short edges of the dust ruffle.

4. Measure your bed from the bottom of the mattress to the floor. Add 5" to this measurement. Trim your long piece of fabric to this measurement.

5. On the bottom edge of the dust ruffle, press under ½"; then press under 4" and stitch in place for a hem. Gather the top edge of the dust ruffle.

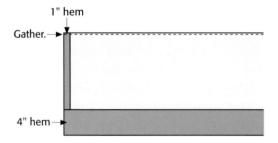

6. Pull up the gathers and adjust them to fit the 2 long sides and width of your bed. Using a ½" seam allowance, sew the dust ruffle to 3 sides of the sheet, distributing the gathers evenly. To prevent the raw edges from fraying, either zigzag the edges or clean finish them with a serger.

SPLIT DUST RUFFLE

If your bed has a footboard, you can get a better fit by making the ruffle in three different parts: one for each of the three sides of the bed. To do this, instead of sewing all the dust ruffle fabric into one long piece, make three individual pieces, each one twice the length of the side of the bed it will cover. Hem both short sides of each individual dust ruffle piece, then sew them to the three sides of the sheet foundation. Now you can fit the dust ruffle nicely around the foot posts without it bunching in the corners.

Quiltmaking Techniques

Refer to this section of the book as needed for information on the basic quiltmaking techniques that will help you complete any of the quilts in this book.

Rotary Cutting

The patchwork pieces for the quilts in this book are cut using a rotary cutter, cutting mat, and acrylic ruler. To straighten the fabric and prepare your fabric for accurate cutting, fold your fabric in half lengthwise with the selvages parallel, on top of the cutting mat. Fold the fabric again, bringing the fold to match the selvages.

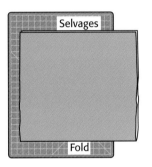
Fabric folded once

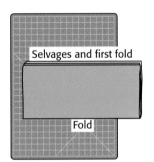
Fabric folded twice

Place a 6" square ruler on the fold nearest you, making sure it is aligned with the fold. Place a larger ruler (6" x 12" or 6" x 24") next to the square so that it covers the uneven edges of the fabric.

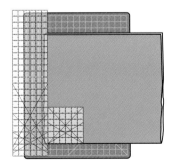
Align rulers.

Hold the long ruler in place, remove the 6" square, and make a clean cut along the edge of the ruler. Roll the rotary cutter away from you, using firm pressure.

Make a clean cut.

Cutting Strips

To cut strips, align the clean-cut edge of the fabric with the ruler marking for the desired strip width and cut a strip.

Cutting Squares or Rectangles

To cut squares or rectangles, cut a strip the desired measurement; then crosscut the strip into the desired shapes.

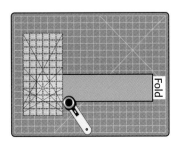

Cutting Triangles

To cut 2 triangles from a square, cut a square the desired measurement. Place the ruler diagonally across the square and cut the square into 2 triangles. These triangles will have the straight of grain on the 2 short legs, and bias along the long diagonal edge.

To cut 4 triangles from a square, cut a square the desired measurement. Cut the square twice diagonally for a total of 4 triangles. These triangles will have the straight of grain along the long edge, and bias edges on the 2 short legs.

Machine Piecing

Many quilters use a sewing machine to sew patchwork, to piece together hand-appliquéd blocks, and to attach borders and binding.

Seam Allowance

The presser foot on your sewing machine is your sewing guide for machine piecing. Many machines have a presser foot that measures ¼" from the stitching line to the right edge of the foot.

To test your machine, sew a sample seam, guiding the cut edge of your fabric into your machine just under the right edge of the foot. Measure the resulting seam allowance. If it's wider or narrower than ¼", adjust how you guide your fabric so that your seams will measure ¼". An easy way to mark an accurate guide is by placing a piece of masking tape on your machine to mark the ¼" seam allowance.

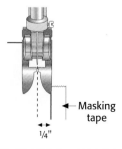

← Masking tape

¼"

Sewing the Pieces Together

Sewing patchwork pieces on the machine can be fun and fast if you "chain piece" the patches into the machine as you sew. Start by sewing the first two patches together. Sew from cut edge to cut edge, using a small stitch length (12–15 stitches per inch). At the end of the seam, stop sewing, but don't cut the thread. Take the next set of patches and feed it into the machine right after the first one. Continue feeding pieces without cutting the thread. When you've sewn all the pieces, clip the thread between the pieces. No wasted thread tails to throw away!

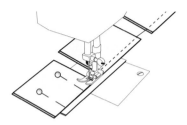

Appliqué Quilts

In an appliqué quilt, appliquéd fabrics are applied on top of other fabrics instead of pieced together to make patchwork patterns. Curved designs can be accomplished easily with appliqué stitches.

Background Fabric

The background fabric for appliqué is usually cut in a square. If the finished size of an appliqué block is 9" square, the block needs to be cut 9½" square to allow for seam allowances. Sometimes it is better to cut the square an inch larger to start and trim it to the correct size after the appliqué has been completed. Appliqué background squares may be cut easily with a large square acrylic ruler and a rotary cutter.

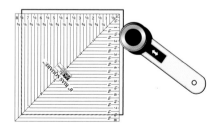

In order to place the appliqué pieces on the background fabric accurately, I like to mark the design on the fabric. Place the fabric right side up over the pattern so that the design is centered. Trace the design carefully. I like to use a silver marking pencil to trace the design. The marks will be dark enough to see and will wash out after the quilt is completed. If your background fabric is too dark and you can't see the pattern clearly, you may need to trace it over a light box or a sunny window.

Preparing Appliqués

Before sewing the appliqué fabrics to the background fabric, you should prepare the appliqués so that the seam allowances are turned under smoothly. This will help you to place the appliqués accurately on the marked background fabric. Use freezer-paper templates to help you make perfectly shaped appliqués.

Freezer-Paper Appliqué

1. Place the freezer paper, plastic-coated side down, on your pattern and trace the design with a sharp pencil. With repeated designs, such as flowers and leaves, make a plastic template and trace around it onto the freezer paper.

2. Cut out the freezer-paper shape on the pencil line. Do not add seam allowances.

3. Place the plastic-coated side of the freezer paper against the wrong side of the appliqué fabric. Iron the freezer paper to the wrong side of the appliqué fabric using a dry, hot iron.

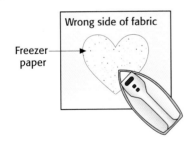

Wrong side of fabric

Freezer paper →

4. Cut out the appliqué shape, adding a ¼"-wide seam allowance around the outside of the freezer paper.

5. Baste the seam allowance over the freezer-paper edges. Clip any inside points, and fold outside points.

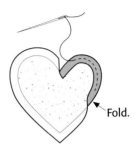

Fold.

6. Pin or baste the appliqué shape to the background fabric.

7. Stitch the appliqué to the background fabric using a traditional appliqué stitch (see page 120 for details).

8. After the shape has been appliquéd, remove any basting stitches. Cut a small slit in the background fabric behind the appliqué and remove the freezer paper with tweezers.

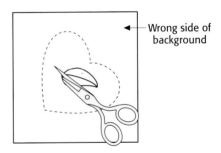

← Wrong side of background

9. Press the appliqué from the wrong side to prevent flattening it too much.

Appliquéd Stems

Bias strips of fabric make great appliqué stems and basket handles. Cut bias strips by measuring an equal distance from a corner of your fabric. Place your ruler on these measurements and make a diagonal cut. Align your ruler with the desired strip width and cut strips.

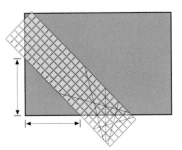

After cutting the bias strips needed, fold the long edges of the strips, wrong sides together, so that they meet in the center of the strips. Baste along the folds using small running stitches.

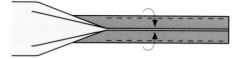

Traditional Appliqué Stitch

The traditional appliqué stitch is appropriate for sewing all areas of appliqué designs, including sharp points and curves.

Start with a single strand of thread approximately 18" long and tie a knot in one end. To hide your knot when you start, slip your needle into the seam allowance from the wrong side of the appliqué piece, bringing it out along the fold line. The knot will be hidden inside the seam allowance.

Stitch along the top edge of the appliqué. If you are right-handed, stitch from right to left. If you are left-handed, stitch from left to right. Start the first stitch by moving your needle straight off the appliqué, inserting the needle into the background fabric.

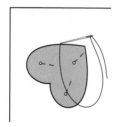

Let the needle travel under the background fabric parallel to the edge of the appliqué, bringing it up about ⅛" away from the last stitch along the pattern line. As you bring the needle back up, pierce the edge of the appliqué piece, catching only one or two threads of the folded edge.

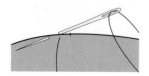

Move the needle straight off the appliqué into the background fabric. Let your needle travel under the background, bringing it up about ⅛" away from the last stitch, again catching the edge of the appliqué. Give the thread a slight tug and continue stitching. The only visible parts of the stitch are very small dots of thread along the appliqué edge.

The part of the stitch that travels forward will be seen as ⅛" stitches on the wrong side of the background fabric. Try to keep the length of your stitches consistent as you stitch along the straight edges. Smaller stitches are sometimes necessary for curves and points.

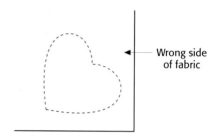

Wrong side of fabric

Quilt Top Assembly

From setting your blocks together to adding borders, you'll find details on assembling your quilt top here.

Squaring Up Blocks

Before you stitch your blocks together, it may be necessary to "square them up" to neaten the edges and make sure they're all the same size. Trim the edges using an acrylic ruler and rotary cutter. Be sure to leave a ¼" seam allowance beyond any points or other important block details near the outside edges of your blocks.

If you cut appliqué blocks larger than the necessary size, trim the blocks square. Use a large square acrylic ruler or cut a square of template plastic the correct size. Draw around the edges of the plastic to indicate the size, then cut with scissors or a rotary cutter on the marked lines. Be sure you've included the ¼" seam allowance all around the outside!

Straight Sets

In straight sets, blocks are laid out in horizontal rows and are parallel to the edges of the quilt. Lay the blocks out on a flat surface. Sew the blocks together in rows; then join the rows to complete the patterned area of the quilt.

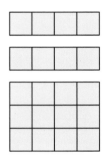

On-Point Sets

Quilts that are set on point are constructed in diagonal rows, with setting triangles added around the edges to complete the corners and sides of the quilt. Lay out all the blocks and setting triangles on a flat surface before you start sewing. Make sure that all blocks are the same size and absolutely square. If you're using plain alternate blocks, they should be exactly the same size as pieced blocks. Arrange the pieces in diagonal rows. Pick up and sew one row at a time, then join the rows to complete the quilt.

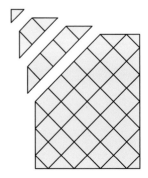

Borders

When the patchwork has been completed and the quilt blocks have been stitched together, borders add a finishing frame to your design. Some of the quilts in this book have borders with overlapped corners, while others have borders with mitered corners.

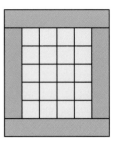 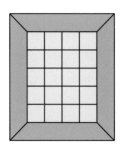

Overlapped Corners   Mitered Corners

Overlapped corners. Two of the borders are cut the size of the inner patchwork design, and the other two borders are cut longer, the length of the total design.

If you are making a large quilt or a quilt with many patchwork pieces, the size of the quilt can vary slightly from the stated size because of all the seams involved. For this reason, it's always a good idea to cut the borders to match your quilt. Check the size by measuring the quilt through the center of the patchwork. Sometimes the edges stretch, and a measurement of the center will be accurate and help you to avoid stretched and rippling borders. Cut the borders according to the center measurement of the quilt. Ease the edge of the quilt to fit the borders.

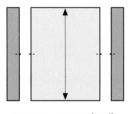

Measure center of quilt,
top to bottom.

To sew the borders, attach the long side borders to the quilt top first. Seams may be pressed toward the border, or pressed to the darker border when adding more than one border.

Then stitch the top and bottom borders, overlapping the two side borders. Press the seam in the same direction as the first borders.

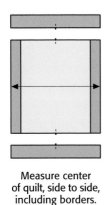

Measure center of quilt, side to side, including borders.

Mitered corners. Estimate the finished outside dimensions of your quilt, including the width of the borders. Cut each border strip at least 1" longer than the required total length.

Fold each border strip in half crosswise and mark the center fold with a pin. Mark the center of each edge of the quilt top. Match the pins on the quilt top with the pins on the border strip. Pin the border strips to the quilt top.

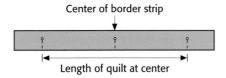

Center of border strip

Length of quilt at center

Sew the border strips to the quilt top, beginning and ending ¼" from the raw edges of the quilt top. Press the seams toward the borders.

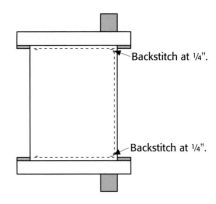

Backstitch at ¼".

Backstitch at ¼".

To miter a corner, lay a corner of the quilt top on a flat surface. Fold one border strip under at a 45° angle. Use a square ruler to check that the corner is flat and square. Press the fold to crease it.

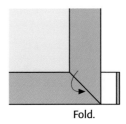

Fold.

Carefully center a piece of 1" masking tape over the mitered fold. The tape will hold your miter in place while you sew the bias seam.

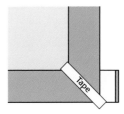

Tape

Open the mitered fold and use a pencil to draw a line on the crease.

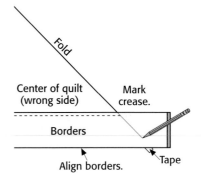

Fold

Center of quilt (wrong side)

Mark crease.

Borders

Align borders.

Tape

Stitch on the pencil line, through the two borders. Remove the tape.

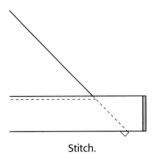

Stitch.

Make sure the seam lies flat on the quilt front and there are no pleats or puckers in the corner where the borders and quilt top meet. Cut away the excess fabric, leaving a ¼" seam, and press the seam open. Repeat for the remaining corners.

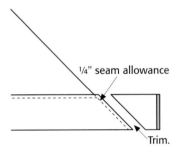

¼" seam allowance

Trim.

Marking the Quilting Designs

Quilting lines can follow the straight lines of patchwork in the quilt, outline the appliqué designs, or embellish spaces between the designs. It may not be necessary to mark quilting designs if you are planning to quilt in the ditch (next to seams) or if you are outlining patchwork pieces.

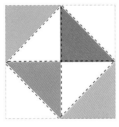
Quilt in the Ditch

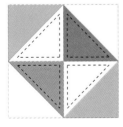
Outline Quilt

For other types of quilting, however, you'll probably want to mark the quilting designs. Do this before basting the three layers together. If the quilt lies flat during the marking process, the lines will be smooth and accurate.

You can use a variety of tools to mark the quilting design onto the quilt top. You can use a regular pencil (#2 or #3), a fine-lead mechanical pencil, a silver marking pencil, or a chalk pencil or chalk marker for dark fabrics. A water-soluble marker can be used to mark the quilting design, but it may disappear before the quilting is completed if your weather is humid. Whichever tool you use for marking, test the tool on a sample of your fabric before using it on your quilt. Make sure you can see the lines, and make sure they can be removed.

To mark straight lines, use a yardstick or a long acrylic ruler. Parallel lines on acrylic rulers will help you keep the lines even. You can also use masking tape to mark straight lines. Simply quilt along the edge of the tape, then peel it off and your markings are removed.

To mark more elaborate quilting designs, place the quilt top on top of the design and trace the design onto the fabric. Use a light box or tape your work against a bright window if you have trouble seeing the design through the fabric. Another way to mark a design is to use a pre-cut plastic quilting stencil, readily available in quilt shops.

Machine quilters often use free-motion designs that do not need to be marked on the fabric.

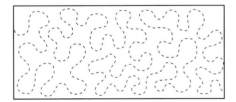

Basting the Layers

Before you begin to quilt, you must baste together the quilt top, batting, and backing. This secures the three layers and keeps the fabrics from slipping throughout the quilting process.

1. Piece together the quilt backing and press it so that it is smooth. Cut the backing at least 2" larger than the quilt top all the way around.

2. Place the backing on a smooth surface, right side down. Use masking tape to fasten the corners and sides of the fabric to the surface.

3. Place the batting on the backing, smoothing it out carefully. If it is very wrinkled, let it relax overnight or fluff it in your clothes dryer for about 15 minutes on the lowest setting before you layer the quilt.

4. Lay the quilt top, right side up, on the batting. Pin the 3 layers together in several places.

5. If you plan to hand quilt, use a long needle and light-colored basting thread. Start in the center and baste a large **X** in the center of the quilt; then baste parallel lines to hold the layers together. The lines should be 4" to 6" apart. The more rows of basting you have, the better your layers will stay together. Baste around the outside edges.

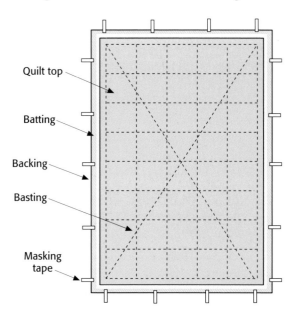

Quilt top

Batting

Backing

Basting

Masking
tape

6. If you plan to machine quilt, use safety pins to baste the layers together at 4" to 6" intervals.

Hand Quilting

Hand quilting stitches are short running stitches used to sew the front, batting, and backing of your quilt together.

1. Thread a Between quilting needle with an 18" length of hand quilting thread and tie a single knot in the long end of the thread. Insert the needle through the top layer of the quilt about ¾" away from the point where you want to start stitching. Slide the needle through the batting layer and bring the needle out at the starting point.

2. Gently tug on the thread until the knot pops through the fabric and is buried in the batting. Take a backstitch and begin quilting, making a small running stitch that goes through all layers. Take 2, 3, or 4 stitches at a time, trying to keep them straight and even.

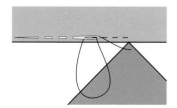

3. To end a line of quilting, make a single knot approximately ¼" from your quilt top. Take one more backstitch into your quilt, tugging the knot into the batting layer and bringing the needle out ¾" away from your stitches. Clip the thread and let the end disappear into your quilt.

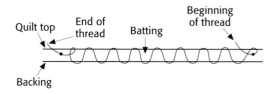

Quilt top   End of   Beginning
                   thread   of thread
                          Batting

Backing

Machine Quilting

Quilts may be quilted quickly by machine. Adjust your stitch length so that it is a little longer than normal, approximately 10 stitches per inch. Test your machine by stitching on a sample quilt sandwich (two layers of fabric with a scrap of batting between them) to make sure that the thread tension is even on the top and bottom.

Straight-Line Quilting

Use a walking foot or even-feed foot on your machine to stitch straight lines, to outline borders, or to quilt in the ditch. A walking foot helps to ease the top and bottom quilt layers evenly through the machine, creating straight lines without puckering.

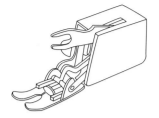

Walking or even-feed foot

Free-Motion Quilting

Free-motion quilting is used to fill in areas or to embellish spaces between patchwork designs. Use this technique to outline a motif or flower in the fabric, to stipple quilt, or to meander around areas in the quilt.

Use a darning foot and lower the feed dogs on your machine so that you can move the fabric in the direction of the design. This technique takes practice or may require a little warm-up time on a sample before you actually sew on your quilt.

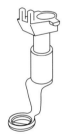

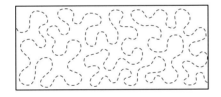

Darning foot

Binding

Binding adds the finishing touch to your quilt. It is usually a good idea to use dark fabrics to frame your design, although if you want your binding to blend in, you can use the same fabric as you use for the outer border. Measure the distance around the quilt and add 10". Cut and sew enough 2"-wide strips of binding fabric to equal this measurement.

Straight-Grain Binding

1. Cut 2"-wide strips across the 42" width of fabric using a rotary cutter and an acrylic ruler.
2. Sew the strips together, using diagonal seams, to create 1 long strip of binding. To make diagonal seams, cross 2 strip ends at right angles, right sides together. Lay these on a flat surface and imagine the strips as a large letter A. Draw a line across the crossed pieces to "cross the A," and then sew along the line. Your seam will be exact, and you can unfold a continuous strip.

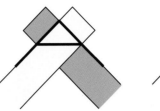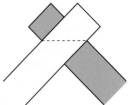

3. Trim the excess fabric, leaving a ¼"-wide seam allowance. Press the seam open to distribute the thickness of the seam.

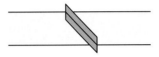

4. Fold the binding strip in half lengthwise, wrong sides together, and press with a hot steam iron.

Applying Binding

1. Machine-baste around the edge of the quilt to securely hold the 3 layers together. Trim any excess threads, batting, or backing even with the front of the quilt.
2. Starting 6" from a corner, align the raw edges of the binding with the raw edges of the quilt. Start sewing 4" from the end of the binding, using a ¼" seam allowance.

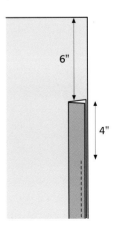

3. To miter the corners of the binding, stop stitching ¼" from the corner and backstitch.

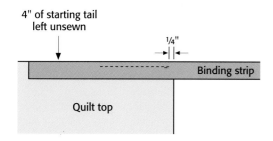

4. Fold the binding diagonally as shown, so that it extends straight up from the second edge of the quilt.

5. Fold the binding down even with the second edge of the quilt. The fold should be even with the first edge. Start sewing the binding ¼" from the fold, making sure to backstitch. Repeat for the remaining corners.

6. To connect the ends of the binding, allow the end to overlap the beginning edge by 2". Cut the end diagonally, with the shortest end of the diagonal on top, nearest to you. Turn the diagonal edge under ¼" and insert the beginning "tail" inside the diagonal fold. Continue sewing the binding onto the quilt.

Turn under ¼" on diagonal end.

Tuck end inside.

7. Fold the binding over the edge of the quilt so it covers the stitching on the back of the quilt. When you fold the corner to the back of the quilt, a folded miter will appear on the front.

On the back, fold one side first, then the other, to create a miter on the back.

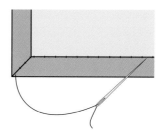

8. Hand stitch the binding to the back of the quilt using the traditional appliqué stitch. Also hand stitch the diagonal fold.

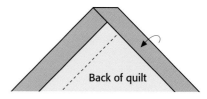

A Label for Your Quilt

You have made a very special quilt. Make a label for the back of your quilt and sign your name and date. You will also want to include information about the quilt: a dedication, group quilt information, or a story about your quilt.

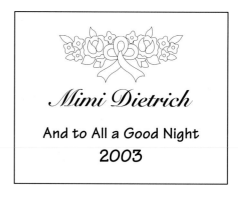

Location Photography

The following bed and breakfast proprietors and homeowners kindly allowed photographs to be taken in their homes and gardens.

THE BENSON FARMSTEAD BED AND BREAKFAST

Shown on pages 16, 82, and 93.
10113 Avon-Allen Road
Bow, WA 98232
800-441-9814
www.bbhost.com/bensonbnb/
Jerry and Sharon Benson, proprietors

THE HERON BED AND BREAKFAST

Shown on pages 36, 54, 60, and 72.
117 Maple Avenue
La Conner, WA 98257
360-466-4626
www.theheron.com
Mike Bruggeman and Gary Kleysteuber, innkeepers

THE WHITE SWAN GUESTHOUSE

Shown on pages 10, 22, 28, 44, and 98.
15872 Moore Road
Mount Vernon, WA 98273
360-445-6805
www.thewhiteswan.com
Peter Goldfarb, proprietor

Photographs were also taken at the home and gardens of Dan and Nancy J. Martin in Kingston, Washington, as shown on pages 66 and 106.

new and bestselling titles from

Martingale™
& C O M P A N Y
America's Best-Loved Craft & Hobby Books™

That Patchwork Place®
America's Best-Loved Quilt Books®

NEW RELEASES
1000 Great Quilt Blocks
American Stenciled Quilts
Americana Quilts
Appliquilt in the Cabin
Bed and Breakfast Quilts
Best of Black Mountain Quilts, The
Beyond the Blocks
Blissful Bath, The
Celebrations!
Color-Blend Appliqué
Fabulous Quilts from Favorite Patterns
Feathers That Fly
Handcrafted Garden Accents
Handprint Quilts
Knitted Throws and More for the Simply
    Beautiful Home
Knitter's Book of Finishing Techniques, The
Knitter's Template, A
Make Room for Christmas Quilts
More Paintbox Knits
Painted Whimsies
Patriotic Little Quilts
Quick Quilts Using Quick Bias
Quick-Change Quilts
Quilts for Mantels and More
Snuggle Up
Split-Diamond Dazzlers
Stack the Deck!
Strips and Strings
Sweet Dreams
Treasury of Rowan Knits, A
Triangle Tricks
Triangle-Free Quilts

APPLIQUÉ
Artful Album Quilts
Artful Appliqué
Blossoms in Winter
Easy Art of Appliqué, The
Fun with Sunbonnet Sue
Sunbonnet Sue All through the Year

BABY QUILTS
Easy Paper-Pieced Baby Quilts
Even More Quilts for Baby
More Quilts for Baby
Play Quilts
Quilted Nursery, The
Quilts for Baby

HOLIDAY QUILTS
Christmas at That Patchwork Place®
Christmas Cats and Dogs
Creepy Crafty Halloween
Handcrafted Christmas, A
Welcome to the North Pole

LEARNING TO QUILT
Joy of Quilting, The
Nickel Quilts
Quick Watercolor Quilts
Quilts from Aunt Amy
Simple Joys of Quilting, The
Your First Quilt Book (or it should be!)

PAPER PIECING
40 Bright and Bold Paper-Pieced Blocks
50 Fabulous Paper-Pieced Stars
For the Birds
Quilter's Ark, A
Rich Traditions

ROTARY CUTTING
101 Fabulous Rotary-Cut Quilts
365 Quilt Blocks a Year Perpetual Calendar
Around the Block Again
Around the Block with Judy Hopkins
Log Cabin Fever
More Fat Quarter Quilts

TOPICS IN QUILTMAKING
Batik Beauties
Frayed-Edge Fun
Log Cabin Fever
Machine Quilting Made Easy
Quick Watercolor Quilts
Reversible Quilts

CRAFTS
300 Papermaking Recipes
ABCs of Making Teddy Bears, The
Creating with Paint
Handcrafted Frames
Painted Chairs
Stamp in Color
Stamp with Style

KNITTING & CROCHET
365 Knitting Stitches a Year Perpetual
    Calendar
Clever Knits
Crochet for Babies and Toddlers
Crocheted Sweaters
Irresistible Knits
Knitted Shawls, Stoles, and Scarves
Knitted Sweaters for Every Season
Knitting with Novelty Yarns
Paintbox Knits
Simply Beautiful Sweaters
Simply Beautiful Sweaters for Men
Too Cute! Cotton Knits for Toddlers
Ultimate Knitter's Guide, The

Our books are available at bookstores and your favorite craft, fabric, and yarn
retailers. If you don't see the title you're looking for, visit us at
www.martingale-pub.com or contact us at:

1-800-426-3126

International: 1-425-483-3313

Fax: 1-425-486-7596

E-mail: info@martingale-pub.com

For more information and a full list of our titles, visit our Web site.